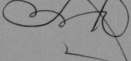

THE TOY & MINIATURE POODLE

Janice Biniok

The Toy & Miniature Poodle

Project Team
Editor: Stephanie Fornino
Copy Editor: Joann Woy
Design: Angela Stanford
Series Design: Stephanie Krautheim and Mada Design
Series Originator: Dominique De Vito

T.F.H. Publications
President/CEO: Glen S. Axelrod
Executive Vice President: Mark E. Johnson
Publisher: Christopher T. Reggio
Production Manager: Kathy Bontz

T.F.H. Publications, Inc.
One TFH Plaza
Third and Union Avenues
Neptune City, NJ 07753

Printed and bound in China
07 08 09 10 11   3 5 7 9 8 6 4

ISBN 978-0-7938-3640-6

Library of Congress Cataloging-in-Publication Data
Biniok, Janice.
  The toy & miniature poodle / Janice Biniok.
     p. cm.
  Includes index.
  ISBN 0-7938-3640-9 (alk. paper)
  1. Miniature poodle. 2. Toy poodle. I. Title: Toy and miniature poodle. II. Title.
  SF429.M57B56 2006
  636.72'8--dc22
  2005035092

This book has been published with the intent to provide accurate and authoritative information in regard to the subject matter within. While every reasonable precaution has been taken in preparation of this book, the author and publisher expressly disclaim responsibility for any errors, omissions, or adverse effects arising from the use or application of the information contained herein. The techniques and suggestions are used at the reader's discretion and are not to be considered a substitute for veterinary care. If you suspect a medical problem consult your veterinarian.

The Leader In Responsible Animal Care For Over 50 Years!®
www.tfh.com

TABLE OF CONTENTS

HISTORY
of the Toy and Miniature Poodle

The Poodle's regal carriage and artistically groomed coat give the impression of an aristocrat of the dog world. It's easy to see why so many people associate the breed with life in the lap of luxury. And while it is true that Toy and Miniature Poodles eventually found favor with the nobility and upper class, a glimpse into the past reveals that Poodles are far more than their appearance suggests.

ORIGINS OF THE BREED

Poodles were originally of the larger (Standard) variety, bred as rugged hunting dogs who excelled at retrieving game fowl from marshes. Ancient Egyptian and Roman artifacts suggest a Poodle-like dog filled such a capacity as far back as 30 CE. But like most dog breeds with a long history, the precise origins of the Poodle are subject to speculation and theory. Some believe the Poodle descended from the North African Barbet, a dog imported to the Iberian Peninsula by the Arabs, and that he eventually dispersed into European countries. He is believed to be closely related to the Portuguese Water Dog and the Irish Water Spaniel, both of whom share many similarities with the Poodle.

The Poodle in Germany

Although Poodles are most often associated with France, historians now say they were originally developed in Germany, where they were used predominantly for hunting. The larger Poodles of this time may have benefited from Russian influences as well. It's important to note that during the breed's development, many different types of Poodles existed, because no set standards were applied to the breed.

Even the name Poodle has German roots, being derived from the German word *Pudel*, meaning *water dog*, or *Pudeln*, which translates as *to splash in water*.

The National Dog of France

The Poodle is the national dog of France, but the breed actually originated in Germany. Poodles were originally bred as water retrievers, and some organizations are reviving this historical purpose by holding retrieving trials for Standard Poodles. Toy and Miniature Poodles were developed later, as companion dogs, and quickly achieved popularity throughout Europe.

Artwork by the famous German artist Albrecht Durer provides evidence that the Poodle had become a popular German breed by the 16th century. During this time, two distinct coat types were distinguished: curly and corded.

Corded dogs sported long, matted cords of hair, resembling dreadlocks, which gave the dog a unique longhaired appearance similar to a Komondor or Hungarian Puli. The cords required meticulous care and had to be oiled to keep the hair supple and prevent breakage. The popularity of the corded coat reached a peak around the turn of the 20th century and then declined. The difficulty in maintaining a corded coat, which was known to harbor dirt and odor, prevented this coat type from becoming very popular for household pets. Corded Poodles were considered a distinct Poodle type even through the early 1900s, but it was later determined that both corded and curly coat types were encompassed within one and the same breed. The corded Poodle, having a very impractical coat to maintain, is now a rare and curious sight.

The Poodle in France

It not known exactly when or how the Poodle first arrived in France, but the first French Poodles were hunting dogs of the larger type, like those used in Germany. This dog, called the *caniche*, was a useful companion for French duck hunters. However, the smaller versions of the Poodle took root here and

The French people greatly contributed to the cultivation of smaller Poodles.

became more refined. It is not known for sure if smaller versions of the Standard Poodle were developed in France or if they arrived from elsewhere, but the French contribution to the cultivation of smaller Poodles cannot be trivialized.

Smaller Poodles became favored companions to the elite during the reigns of Louis XIV and Louis XV. The Poodle was further miniaturized during the reign of Louis XVI to become the toy-size Poodle who so enamored the nobility of the time. Exactly what breeding was used to produce the smaller size Poodles is unknown, but it is speculated that the Toy Poodle may have been infused with the genetic contribution of a small white dog from Malta, now called the Maltese.

Poodle Sizes

Toy and Miniature Poodles were bred down from the Standard size, the Standard being the oldest of the three sizes. However, all three sizes are considered to be one breed. No physical or temperamental distinctions exist among them.

Easier to care for and more practical as household companions, miniaturized Poodles, known as *petit barbets* in France, became prevalently known as the French Poodle to the rest of the world. (This name is still commonly used to refer to both Toy and Miniature Poodles.) The Poodle's sparkling intelligence, boundless affection, and unique physical characteristics endeared him to the people of France so much so that he became the national dog of that country.

POPULARIZATION IN EUROPE

Historical accounts often neglect to give enough credit to the performing dogs who helped popularize the Poodle throughout the European continent. Traveling circuses began to emerge in the early 1800s, and trained animals were added as feature attractions by 1830. Poodles quickly found their place as entertainers within this new industry. Around the same time, a number of trained dog troupes began to travel throughout Europe, showcasing the amazing abilities of the Poodle.

A showman named Crawley maintained a troupe of highly trained Poodles called *The Ball of Little Dogs*, which performed in London and surrounding areas. Queen Anne of England was said to be completely smitten by their performance, which involved dogs dancing in rhythm to music. Poodle performances were also documented in France, Italy, and Germany during the 19th century. In *A History and Description of*

All three Poodle sizes are considered to be one breed.

the *Modern Dogs of Great Britain and Ireland* (1894), Rawdon B. Lee remarks, "As I write, I should say there are now in 1893, at least half-a-dozen troupes of performing dogs in the metropolis, and each contains several Poodles."

Because language barriers do not necessarily inhibit such forms of entertainment, circuses and trained-dog troupes often traveled internationally, contributing to the Poodle's notoriety throughout Europe. The Poodle's intelligence, agility, and unusually frilly coat had indeed inspired many to become starstruck by this remarkable breed. The feats of these incredible performing dogs were the talk of the age, and amazement gave birth to admiration.

The creative grooming of these performing Poodles also may have piqued the imagination of Poodle owners of the time.

The Multi-Talented Poodle

The versatility of these intelligent and athletic dogs allowed them to develop and fulfill a number of purposes during their dispersion throughout Europe. In addition to serving as a beloved companion animal, the toy variety became popular hand warmers in Europe around the time of the Renaissance, when small dogs were often kept within the stylishly large sleeves of their owners and referred to as *sleeve dogs*. Traveling gypsies and circuses recognized the Poodle's talented capabilities as a performer and utilized his curly coat as a medium for showy adornment. During the 19th century, Poodles also found employment as truffle hunters, used to sniff out the valuable fungal delicacy used in European cuisine.

When the nobility and upper class realized the Poodle's luxuriously thick and fluffy coat could be clipped and decorated in an endless number of fashionable styles, the fine art of Poodle grooming was born. Even so, many popular Poodle clips used today still are based on historically utilitarian purposes. Fluffs of fur that appear to be nothing more than ornamentation are actually grooming techniques derived from the Poodle's hunting heritage. Pompons placed on hips and legs protected the joints from cold water and abrasions. A thick coat left on the dog's chest and thorax provided protection and warmth for vital organs. Shaved areas on the hindquarters and legs reduced resistance and allowed the dog to swim and move freely in the environment in which he was required to work. Even the colorful ribbons tied to a Poodle's topknot (hair on the top of the head) may have had historical significance as a method of identifying individual dogs while hunting.

THE POODLE IN ENGLAND

After the Napoleonic Wars, soldiers returning from Germany and France brought a large number of Poodles back to England, where they became regular competitors in the show ring by 1880. The first Poodle was registered with the Kennel Club (KC) in 1874, and the Curly Poodle Club of England was founded in 1876.

Initially, Poodles entering show competition were grouped together regardless of size or coat type. Not until 1910 were curly and corded Poodles classed in separate divisions and smaller Poodles judged in a class of their own. All smaller Poodles were classed as Miniatures until the Toy Poodle finally received individual recognition from world breed clubs after 1940.

THE POODLE IN THE UNITED STATES

No one knows when the first Poodles arrived in the United States, but they most likely carried English bloodlines. The American Kennel Club (AKC) registered its first Poodle in 1887, but a formal standard for the breed was not established until after the formation of the Poodle Club of America. Interestingly, this club was originally founded in 1896, but disbanded shortly after due to a lack of interest and support. The popularity of the Poodle in America declined significantly in the early 1900s, almost to the point of causing the breed to die out in the United States. This wane in popularity is perplexing, considering that the Poodle had become well known to Americans by then. The Poodle already had a reputation as a talented circus performer, had endeared himself to American children with the publication of the very popular children's book *Little Women* before the turn of the century, and had been used as an image of elegance on postcards and other printed media in America by the 1920s.

The Kennel Club (KC)

The KC was founded in Great Britain, in 1873, as a way to provide central governance for dog shows and other canine matters. A studbook was compiled, and rules and regulations were established, many of which became the foundation for kennel clubs in other countries.

The KC registers an average of 260,000 dogs per year. Approximately 200 breeds of dogs are eligible for registration and are classified under seven groups: hounds, gundogs, terriers, utility, working, pastoral, and toys. In 1985, the KC established a library that has become the largest collection of canine information sources in Europe.

The KC's interest in dogs has broadened over the years to include canine health, legislative issues, and responsible dog ownership. As a way of addressing the needs of all dogs and their owners, and to help fulfill its mission statement to promote the general improvement of the dog, the KC allows the registration of mixed-breed dogs within its activity register and with its Companion Dog Club. These dogs are eligible to participate in special classes offered at Companion Dog Shows.

The American Kennel Club (AKC)

The AKC is a not-for-profit organization founded in the United States in 1884 for the purpose of maintaining a registry for purebred dogs and sanctioning dog events that promote the breeding of purebred dogs for type and function. Like the KC, its interest in dogs has expanded throughout the years to include support for responsible dog ownership, public education, canine health, and canine welfare issues.

The AKC registers over 1 million dogs and sponsors more than 15,000 dog competitions each year. Currently, 150 different breeds are registered by the club, and they are assigned to seven groups not including the Miscellaneous Class. These seven groups are based on the original purpose for which the dogs were used and include sporting dogs, hounds, terriers, working dogs, herding dogs, toys, and nonsporting dogs. The AKC also maintains one of the world's largest libraries devoted to dogs, which was established in 1934.

It wasn't until 1931 that the Poodle Club of America reformed and became an effective entity. Not long after that, the first Poodle won the Best in Show award at Westminster, in 1935. This honor was bestowed on International Champion Nunsoe Duc de La Terrace of Blakeen, an imported, white Standard dog whose achievements in the show ring have been attributed to generating serious interest in the breed in America.

As the most prestigious dog show in America, Westminster offers the most coveted awards in the world of American dog fancy, and Poodles have repeatedly reached the peak of success. The Miniature Poodle made his mark at Westminster with a Best in Show in 1943, and the Toy finally achieved this distinction in 1956. Since then, Poodles from each size category have frequented the top of the award list, including the most recent and electrifying Best in Show win of the Miniature Poodle Ch. Surrey Spice Girl in 2002.

Just as prestigious on the English front is the Crufts dog show, where Poodles have also done very well for themselves. With the first show debuting in 1891, Crufts became world famous by the early 1900s. Five Best in Show wins have been awarded to Standard and Toy Poodles at Crufts since 1955, with the only Poodle inexplicably lacking on this honor roll being the Miniature.

Although the Poodle's popularity remained relatively static during World War II, interest in Poodles surged in England after the war, a trend that was mirrored in the United States. Popularity reached a peak in England by the 1950s, and its status in America followed suit by the 1960s. Poodles were in high demand during this time, much to the detriment of the breed. This surge in popularity caused some problems for the breed, because it encouraged indiscriminate breeding that resulted in genetic temperament and physical faults.

Some of the problems that plagued the breed included nervous or neurotic dispositions, unstable patellas, and ingrown eyelashes. Fortunately, the Poodle's population boom finally abated, along with the proliferation of such faults, and the breed has improved considerably. Its popularity, however, has continued to maintain a high rank ever since. The Poodle remained the single most popular breed of dog in America for more than two decades, from 1960 to 1983. Today, the Poodle continues to place within the top ten breeds in popularity in the United States, according to registration statistics provided by the AKC.

Throughout history, the Poodle has been a jack-of-all-trades, filling various roles and successfully performing just about any duties presented to him. Today, he serves as companion, service dog, therapy dog, entertainer, and watchdog, among other capacities. He is associated with glamour but is abundant with practicality. Fun for children and an incomparable source of companionship for the elderly, the Poodle is not restricted to any particular niche, but finds his place with people from all walks of life.

Famous Poodle Owners

Poodles have found favor with a number of influential and notable people throughout history, including Beethoven and Chopin, who were known to be Poodle lovers. Winston Churchill, most often associated with English Bulldogs, had a special place in his heart for his Miniature Poodle, Rufus. When Rufus suffered an untimely and tragic death after being hit by a car, he was subsequently replaced by another Miniature Poodle named Rufus II.

Despite the Poodle's reputation as a spoiled canine, the breed is intelligent, lively, and courageous.

2

CHARACTERISTICS
of the Toy and Miniature Poodle

M any people are initially attracted to Toy and Miniature Poodles because they are small, adorable, and physically unique, but what begins as an outer attraction eventually becomes a respect and appreciation for the Poodle's inner beauty—his intelligence, devotion, and sensitivity. This combination of physical and temperamental traits paints a true picture of the whole dog, with some believing that the Poodle makes one of the most delightful character portraits in the canine kingdom.

PHYSICAL CHARACTERISTICS

Toy and Miniature Poodles may look identical in most respects—their conformation, coats, and colors are the same—but size does influence some personality traits and may also determine whether one or the other will make a suitable pet for a particular family situation.

Height and Weight

As mentioned earlier, Toy and Miniature Poodles have the same general physical characteristics except that of size. The breed standards for both the American Kennel Club (AKC) and Kennel Club (KC) are almost identical in this respect, with the Miniature Poodle measuring more than 10 inches (25.4 cm) up to 15 inches (38.1 cm) high at the highest point of the shoulders and the Toy Poodle measuring 10 inches (25.4 cm) or under. Weight should be proportionate to height, with Miniature Poodles running between 12 (5.4 kg) and 18 lbs (8.2 kg) and Toy Poodles between 6 (2.7 kg) and 9 lbs (4.1 kg).

Some European countries recognize four different size standards for the Poodle that include a classification for "dwarfs" between 11 (27.9 cm) and 13.75 inches (34.9 cm). The KC, however, does not recognize this size, and dogs falling within that height range are considered Miniatures. Similarly, in the United States, it is common to see advertisements for Teacup Poodles, which is not a size recognized by the AKC. These are actually very tiny Toy Poodles who have been bred down in size to meet

What Is a Breed Standard?

A breed standard is a scale by which all specimens of a particular breed may be measured. The standard reflects the physical and sometimes temperamental traits that all breeders should strive to obtain from their breeding efforts. There probably isn't a dog worthy enough to fulfill every requirement of a standard, because the standard is based on what is perceived to be a perfect specimen. Judges use the standard as a guide when evaluating dogs at a dog show, and those who come closest to meeting each requirement of the standard are awarded.

the market demand for ever-smaller Poodles. In the process of miniaturization, Teacup Poodles have been known to experience a plethora of health problems and genetic defects, making them inferior representations of the breed.

When reviewing the physical description of a Poodle, it's easy to see how almost every feature contributes to the Poodle's image of a refined creature. His overall appearance should model elegance and gaiety, and his well-proportioned body should be completely free of exaggeration.

Head

Suitable specimens of the breed will have a finely chiseled head and face, with a skull that is not too round or broad. The features of the face should be strong, with flat cheekbones and a well-defined chin that is not undershot or protruding. The Poodle's pleasingly attractive facial features are accented by a long, straight muzzle and tight-fitting lips. The teeth conform to this functional shape by being set in a snug scissor bite, with the upper teeth properly overlapping the lower teeth.

The tight construction of the Poodle does not allow any excess skin to create folds or wrinkles. The skin should be snug at the neck, without any indication of dewlaps. There should be no rolling of the skin at the base of the neck or the base of the tail. This contributes to the Poodle's sleek form, a quality that becomes even more pronounced by the Poodle's high, dignified head carriage. The neck must be long enough to rise into the graceful set of the head.

The Poodle's overall appearance should model elegance and gaiety.

Eyes

The Poodle's eyes should offer a clear indication of his

intelligence. They are oval in shape and wide-set, offering plenty of space for brain capacity. A Poodle with small, narrow eyes does not possess the physical traits necessary to project the image of an intellectual canine. Eyes that are too round, too large, or the wrong color deviate from the standard.

The Poodle should have a finely chiseled face and head.

Ears

This sharp vision of elegance is not harmed by the Poodle's soft, pendulous ears, as they hang low and close to the face. When the ears are too short or set too high, they tend to jut out from the head and break the smooth lines of the Poodle's profile. Correct ear placement, sufficient thickness to the ear leather, and adequate substance to the fur help prevent "fly-away" ears, which are an unattractive fault.

Tail

The tail is carried high, almost erect, with a slight slant away from the body, and it is customarily docked to about half its length or a little shorter. The KC standards offer a description of undocked tails, stating that they should be set high, carried away from the body, and held as straight as possible. But the AKC expects all tails to be docked.

Body Type and Structure

The balance of the Poodle's frame is supported by shoulders that slant across the neck toward the withers, and hindquarters that complement the angle of the shoulders. Both the front and rear legs should be straight, with the hocks and feet turning neither inward nor outward. Any deviation from these proportions will impair the Poodle's balance and negatively affect his eloquent outline.

Consistent with these proportions and the Poodle's athletic ability, the Poodle is deep chested, with well-sprung ribs, and he has smooth but pronounced muscling throughout.

Other than a slight hollow just behind the shoulders, the back should be short and straight.

The physical characteristics contributing to the Poodle's lean, well-balanced structure also contribute to his outstanding athletic abilities. Few breeds of dog are known to possess as much coordination in performing physical feats—thus the popularity of Poodles in circuses and other forms of entertainment. The Poodle is built squarely and symmetrically, which gives him a stable form with which to execute typically difficult maneuvers. Anyone who has trained a Poodle to do tricks is amazed at the ease with which he can learn to accomplish spins, leaps, and flips. Poodles are undeniably the most impressive gymnasts of the canine world.

European Size Standards

Some European countries have established different size standards for Poodles that include four different size descriptions not recognized by the KC or the AKC. These sizes include:

- Standards at 18.75 inches (47.6 cm) or taller at the shoulders
- Miniatures at 13.75 (34.9 cm) to 18.75 inches (47.6 cm)
- Dwarfs at 11 (27.9 cm) to 13.75 inches (34.9 cm)
- Toys up to 11 inches (27.9 cm)

Gait

The Poodle's conformation gives him a natural elegance. With a light, springy gait, he displays exceptional grace. Poodles have, as

The Poodle has a lean, well-balanced structure.

the AKC standard describes it, "an air of distinction and dignity." This also indicates that the Poodle's attitude and personality are manifest in his carriage.

Coat

The external physical characteristic that obviously sets the Poodle apart from most other breeds is his curly coat. The coat should be dense, with a harsh texture, resembling the fleece of a lamb's wool. It will have very tight curls or ringlets when left unbrushed and a fluffy appearance when properly dried and brushed. This unusual hair type has some unique characteristics.

Characteristics of Poodle Hair

The Poodle's hair does not shed out in the usual manner. Due to the structure of the hair, loose hair and dander tend to be retained in the coat until it is brushed out. This makes the Poodle a very desirable house pet, because little, if any, hair is left on carpets, furniture, or clothing. It is also a beneficial trait for allergy sufferers, and many consider the Poodle a hypoallergenic breed. Whether a Poodle is a suitable pet for an individual allergic to dogs depends on a number of factors, such as the allergy-sufferer's sensitivity and what other steps are taken to minimize reactions. But for some who would otherwise not be able to own a dog because of allergies, Poodles are a fine consideration.

In addition, most dogs have hair that grows to a certain length, but Poodle hair never stops growing. This continuously growing coat will grow to unmanageable lengths if it is not trimmed regularly. Hair even grows within the ear canals and can accumulate to the point of causing ear infections and hearing problems. This hair is usually plucked out regularly during the grooming process.

Breed Profile		
Height		Toy Poodle—under 10 inches (25.4 cm)
		Miniature Poodle—over 10 inches (25.4 cm) up to 15 inches (38.1 cm)
Weight (kg)		Toy Poodle—6 (2.7 kg) to 9 pounds (4.1 kg)
		Miniature Poodle—12 (5.4 kg) to 18 pounds (8.2 kg)
Life Expectancy		14 to 16 years
Coat		Color: Solid colors only. White, cream, brown, apricot, red, black, silver, blue, and café-au-lait
Hypoallergenic		Yes
Shedding		Minimal, if any, shedding
Grooming		Daily brushing; clipping every six weeks
Drooling		None
Minimum Accommodations		Apartment with or without a yard
Energy Level		Moderate to high
Exercise Time		20 to 40 minutes per day
Trainability		Learns quickly
Protective		Moderate

A lack of grooming care for a Poodle can result in a profusion of mats and an overabundance of hair serious enough to cause health problems. The mats of an unkempt Poodle can become very large, heavy, and debilitating. Mats that become very tight and close to the skin can actually begin to tear at the skin, and mats between the foot pads and toes can cause sores and difficulty walking. An excessive accumulation of hair is prone to harbor fleas, ticks, dirt, and contaminants that are not easily removed due to the thickness and depth of the hair.

Maintaining a Poodle's coat involves a considerable expense and time commitment, whether the owner decides to use the services of a professional groomer or invest in the necessary equipment to perform the grooming herself. This should be an important consideration when deciding to own a Poodle.

Hair Styles

Dogs in the show ring are required to have their hair clipped in traditional styles, usually the English Saddle Clip or the Continental Clip. The English Saddle Clip involves clipping short the face, feet, base of the tail, and portions of the legs and midsection. Two pompons are left on the rear legs, one on each front leg, and one on the tip of the tail. The mane, ears,

and topknot are left long, while a shorter blanket of hair is trimmed on the hindquarters. This type of clip takes many hours with an experienced hand.

The Continental Clip is very similar to the English Saddle Clip, save for the treatment of the hindquarters. The hindquarters are shaved to leave a rosette on each hip, and only one pompon is left on each rear leg. The AKC allows puppies under a year old

Although most dogs have hair that only grows to a certain length, Poodle hair never stops growing.

to be shown in a Puppy Clip, which is a simpler type of clip consisting of shaved face, throat, feet, and base of tail, and an even clip over the rest of the body. The tail pompon is the only embellishment on the Puppy Clip.

The high-maintenance show clips are not very practical for household pets, because they require constant brushing, cleaning, and wrapping to keep them clean and looking good. Fortunately, endless other options are available to pet owners. For those who truly wish to display their dogs in one of the traditional show styles, the option exists for having the dog trimmed into a shorter, easier-to-maintain version. Although grooming is a very large responsibility in Poodle ownership, it is also the fun part of owning this breed, because pet dogs can be shorn in any style that meets their owners' tastes.

The Poodle's coat can become a creative outlet with which his owner can project any image she desires. From a simple puppy clip to an outrageous sculpture in fur, the Poodle often becomes a canvas for personal expression. Poodles definitely do not need to be groomed to portray the feminine image that tends to characterize the breed. Although most Poodle owners prefer a short, simple clip for practical reasons, it doesn't hurt to keep an open mind to the possibilities!

Coat Colors

The choices available to Poodle owners are not restricted to grooming preferences, because the Poodle offers a great variety of colors to consider. Breed standards require all of the following colors to be solid: white, cream, brown, apricot, red, black, silver, and blue. The AKC recognizes a color called "café-au-lait" (light brown), which is not listed in the KC standard, and the KC standard includes requirements for reds, which are not mentioned in the AKC standard. Interestingly, some Poodles are not born the same color they will attain by adulthood. Silvers are usually born black and eventually fade to a silver color with age. Browns, apricots, and reds also are born with a deeper shade of fur than they will display as adults.

Coat color determines the color of the eyes, toenails, lips, and

Silver-colored Poodles are usually born black and eventually fade to a silver color with age.

eye rims. Brown and café-au-lait Poodles should have dark amber eyes, dark toenails, and liver-colored noses, eye-rims, and lips. Black, blue, gray, silver, apricot, cream, and white Poodles should have very dark eyes and black toenails, noses, eye-rims, and lips. The AKC allows apricot Poodles to have amber eyes and liver-colored noses, eye-rims, and lips, but this is not a desirable color combination. The KC allows both apricots and reds to have deep amber eyes and liver-colored points.

Parti-colored Poodles are not an acceptable color, according to breed standards, because they are not solid colored. These Poodles display a color pattern involving more than one color, such as a white dog with black patches. A movement has begun to promote parti-colored Poodles as a distinct Poodle type, and although they are not currently allowed in the show ring, their unique coloring has found favor in the pet market.

The coat that makes a Poodle so outwardly unique provides other advantages for Poodle owners. Poodles are relatively clean dogs when groomed well, and they do not have the "doggy odor" attributed to some breeds. People find themselves attracted to the Poodle because his coat is so tempting to touch. As a conversation piece, they stimulate social interactions and provide opportunities to meet people. Poodle owners always seem to have interesting and entertaining stories to tell about their distinctive canine companions.

IS THE TOY OR MINI POODLE RIGHT FOR YOU?

Toy and Miniature Poodles make excellent pets for the majority of those who own them. They are very versatile and possess many qualities desired of a pet, but it is still important to consider their specific needs to determine if this breed is right for you.

Activity Level

Some sources indicate that the Poodle has a moderate activity level, while others claim that he is a high-energy dog. Why the discrepancy? Because dogs, like people, are individuals. The DNA that makes all Poodles similar also makes each one a little different. As a result, a trait like activity level really comprises a range of needs.

The majority of Poodles actually fall somewhere between moderate and high activity levels. Whether a dog falls at either end of that spectrum or somewhere in between depends entirely on genetics. One thing is for certain: Poodles are active dogs. A Poodle will not be content to lie at your feet or curl up in front of a fireplace for hours at a time. A very sedate Poodle is probably a very sick one.

Poodle Temperament

It would be difficult to find a properly raised Poodle who displays a sour attitude, meanness, or a lack of self-esteem. Poodles have a sense of pride. Although some people describe them as vain, aloof, and haughty, the truth is that they are smart, and they know it. For centuries, Poodles have been praised as one of the most intelligent dog breeds in the world, and it would be unnatural for them to hide such a predominant quality. Dogs in the show ring are expected to publicly display their good nature and superior intellect.

It is important to consider what kind of activity level you are willing to provide in terms of play and exercise when deciding to own a Poodle. For the moderate-level dog, 20 minutes of exercise per day should be enough to keep him happy and healthy. High-level dogs will require at least 30 minutes per day. Fortunately, Poodles do not require outdoor exercise if they can receive enough exercise indoors.

Toy and Mini Poodles make excellent pets for the majority of those who own them.

True to his lively personality, the Poodle can easily become very excited in some situations. When he knows it is time for outside play or a walk, his fervent display of spins and jumps can be quite amusing. However, it becomes a little annoying when he jumps excitedly on arriving guests, and his owner may need to use some patience and training to help him control his exuberance when company calls.

Affinity for Children and Other Pets

Poodles, in general, have wonderful dispositions with children. It's not their temperament that needs to be considered as much as their size when determining if a Poodle will make a suitable pet for families with children. Depending on the age of the children and what size Poodle is desired, certain recommendations are in order.

Children under the age of five must be highly supervised with any pet. They are very curious about animals at this age and often interact with them in inappropriate ways. Because Toy and Miniature Poodles are so small, they are enticing targets for young children. Unfortunately, they are also easily injured. Any animal, no matter how docile, is inclined to defend itself when put in a threatening position. While larger dogs have the strength to pull away from a young child's grasp, Toy and Miniature Poodles do not. For these reasons, Toy and Miniature Poodles are not usually recommended for families with very young children.

Miniature Poodles can make wonderful playmates for children over the age of five, provided the children receive adequate supervision. A Poodle's energy and love for play are a perfect match for older children who are taught how to handle pets properly.

The Toy Poodle, however, is not recommended for families with children under ten years of age. Like other diminutive breeds, Toy Poodles require gentle

Children, especially very young children, should be highly supervised around Poodles.

handling. Younger children may not have the maturity, coordination, or pet-handling skills to treat a Toy Poodle with the light hand he requires.

Regarding other pets, Toy and Miniature Poodles do well with other dogs and most other pets, as long as they are properly introduced. Again, though, their small size should be considered. Pairing a Toy Poodle with a large, boisterous dog could mean injuries for the smaller one.

Attention Requirement

Toy and Miniature Poodles desire a great deal of human interaction, perhaps because they seem to think in human terms. On the other hand, it may be that the strong devotion they have for their owners creates such an emotional attachment. In either case, the Poodle demands a lot of attention. He does not like to be separated from his owner or left alone.

The demand for attention may be more than some people want, while others relish the close bond such a demand creates. Having a pet who obviously needs us provides emotional and health benefits in the form of giving us purpose, making us feel needed, and keeping us active. Those who are too busy to meet a Poodle's demand for attention, however, may face problem behaviors. It is important for you to want a dog who is interested in everything you do and everywhere you go, and you should make sure you have the time to give the dog the attention he craves. Those who are willing to make the sacrifice of time and attention will have the opportunity to develop one of the closest human–canine relationships possible.

Cleanliness

Toy and Miniature Poodles are exceptionally clean dogs. In

Children and Dogs

The following are some general guidelines for parents regarding children and pets:

1. Supervise children under the age of ten when they are around pets.

2. Teach children not to play with a pet's extremities, although you can encourage body petting and other appropriate interactions.

3. Set a good example by not interacting too roughly with a pet in front of your children.

4. Ask your children to help with pet chores, such as feeding or picking up pet toys. Taking care of a family pet is much more fun when it becomes a team effort for all members of the family. Never make children solely responsible for the dog's care. The parents should be the dog's primary caretaker.

5. Give pets living in a household with young, active children a safe escape away from the children, where they can retreat from noise and activity. A gated room or a dog crate located in a quiet area of the home can provide refuge for the dog who needs time alone.

6. Teach pets living in a household with a very young child to retreat if the child makes inappropriate advances. This will help avoid dangerous confrontations.

addition to their nearly shedless coats, they are relatively neat eaters and do not drool. If raised in a clean environment, they learn to prefer cleanliness. Although they can get into mischief occasionally, they are not heavy chewers and are not capable of wreaking the degree of destruction a larger dog could.

Hardiness

Poodles are a hardy breed of dog, and they are suitable for just about any climate. Lengthening or shortening the coat can help the Poodle tolerate temperature extremes, so few places in the world exist to which he cannot adjust. The Poodle is not, however, an outdoor dog. His devotion to his owner and desire for attention is too great to tolerate separate living arrangements. A Poodle will settle for nothing less than being a member of the family.

Intelligence

The Poodle's intelligence, although a desirable attribute, can create challenges. Similar to other dogs known to have an active mind, Poodles require plenty of attention and mental activity. Like a gifted child in a remedial program, they become bored and troublesome without adequate mental stimulation.

Boredom often can take the form of mischievousness. A Poodle might purposely engage in an inappropriate activity as a way of communicating that he needs more attention. This can be both annoying and endearing, because the Poodle tends to do

Because Poodles are so intelligent, they require plenty of attention and mental activity.

such things with a sense of humor—a soggy dog toy dropped strategically in the middle of your newspaper or hiding one of your shoes behind the couch. Poodle owners who learn to appreciate these behaviors for what they are—displays of intelligence—will be better equipped to deal with them appropriately. Never discipline a Poodle for using his mind; instead, direct him to a more acceptable activity.

Although Poodles can be very active, they do not require large indoor or outdoor living spaces.

Living Space

Although Poodles can be highly active, they do not require large indoor or outdoor spaces in which to expend their energy. The Poodle actually requires very little living space, and he is content even in an apartment with little or no yard. Lots of time and attention, not living space, will keep a Poodle happy. This is one reason why Poodles have become so popular as pets—a Poodle can tolerate almost any type of accommodation, both large and small, provided his other needs are met.

The Poodle's ability to live in smaller surroundings, in combination with his desire to be with his owner, makes him a wonderful traveling companion. Living within the confines of a motor home or hotel room causes few problems for the Toy or Miniature Poodle, and he makes a good choice for retirees who like to travel. People with careers that entail a lot of travel will also do well with a Toy or Miniature Poodle. Their small size and clean habits make them acceptable at hotels that otherwise wouldn't allow dogs, and they can be easily transported in carriers on planes, buses, and other modes of transportation.

Longevity

Known for his longevity, the Poodle outlives many other

breeds of dog. The average life span for Toy and Miniature Poodles is 14 to 16 years, which provides Poodle owners with many years of companionship. These smaller Poodles are not considered aged until the age of 10, although some signs of aging may creep up before that time. It is not unusual for them to display youthful behavior well into their senior years.

Personality

Poodles are very sensitive and perceptive. Poodle owners quickly realize that they cannot fool their canine friend, for this very observant dog can detect any subtle hint of body language or change in voice tone.

Emotivity

Some people classify Poodles as emotional beings. In fact, Poodles often are described as having human-like qualities and have been referred to as "people in curly suits." This is not surprising, because Poodles, as far as canines are concerned,

Poodles are very devoted to those they love.

are masters of communication. They have an uncanny ability to read and respond to body language. They can tell instantly if you are sad, and they rejoice with all the exuberance that is Poodle when you are happy.

Their intuitiveness can be so astounding that some owners wonder if their pet could be telepathic. Such a quality creates a very strong bond between the Poodle and his owner, and Poodles are indeed very devoted to those they love. Intuition also enables the Poodle to provide great comfort for those who need it. This sensitivity to human emotions makes them a wonderful choice as therapy dogs.

So sensitive are some Poodles that extremely stressful situations can actually cause physical illness. Poodles do not do well in homes plagued with family tension, loud altercations, or emotional outbursts. An environment filled with conflict can cause digestive upsets or lead to neurotic behaviors. The Poodle requires a harmonious, emotionally stable home.

Did You Know?

Poodles are extremely sensitive and perceptive, and they are able to detect subtle body language and changes in voice tone.

Desire to Please

The Poodle rewards his owner with a strong desire to please and an abundance of affection. Full of cuddles and kisses, his puppy-like personality is entertaining and uplifting. Poodles are very happy dogs with upbeat attitudes, and they are often described as having *joie de vivre*. Poodle owners find themselves turning off the television to watch the amusing antics of their little canine clowns, because Poodles find immense pleasure in generating laughter.

Friendliness

Poodles are generally friendly dogs, and while they can be somewhat cautious of strangers, they should not be unpredictably aggressive or excessively fearful. Some Poodles who exhibit personality faults because of overbreeding and inbreeding still exist, an undesirable effect of the breed's popularity. Exercise caution in the purchase of a Poodle to avoid those who are overly high-strung, nervous, or timid. Poodle buyers should insist on meeting both the sire and dam, if possible, when purchasing a Poodle puppy. This will give a good indication of what kind of personality traits a puppy will inherit.

Nippiness

The Poodle can be a naturally cautious dog, and he needs socialization to avoid developing problems with shyness and timidity. Exposing the dog to many different sights, sounds, people, and other dogs at a young age will give him the opportunity to develop trust and confidence that will benefit him throughout his life. This is not a difficult task given the size and portability of Toy and Miniature Poodles, and it is a recommended element in raising any type of dog. Without this exposure, Toy Poodles in particular are prone to becoming suspicious, or worse, developing the bad habit of defensive biting.

In fact, Toy Poodles have received a bad rap when it comes to nippiness, but this is sometimes more a product of environment than genetics. Being content to spend most of his time indoors, a Toy Poodle who has become accustomed to such a limited territory and who has had a lack of outside social experiences will not have the opportunity to develop good social skills. He also may become possessive of his owner, his food, or his toys. As a result, it is very important to socialize these dogs at a young age and provide the necessary training to address problems with nippiness and possessiveness as soon as they appear.

Protectiveness

Although not known to be exceptionally protective, Toy and Miniature Poodles are very devoted and faithful to their owners and may attempt to protect them if the situation arises. The combination of a perceptive nature and keen intelligence provides the Poodle with the capacity for sound judgment. He can sense when his family is in danger. He should not be aggressive, however, and any inappropriate aggressiveness should be resolved with socialization and training. Poodles are not dominant dogs; instead, they strike a good balance between dominance and submission.

The Poodle is also a very alert dog, and as such, he makes a wonderful watchdog. Few things escape his watchful eye and attentive ears. He will not hesitate to let you know when company arrives or if anything is amiss. The Poodle enjoys this job immensely, although it also causes some problems with his reputation. Sometimes referred to as *yappers*, Poodles do enjoy communicating, whether vocally or otherwise, and it is true that some Poodles perhaps get a little too much pleasure out of it. But like other traits based on instinct or predisposition, it can be controlled.

Trainability

For dog owners, the Poodle's outstanding level of intelligence means that he is easy to train. Toy and Miniature Poodles learn quickly, and they have a great memory. They are also relatively easy to housetrain, and they excel at obedience training. This intelligence, boosted by a strong desire to please, means that the Poodle does not require a firm hand in training, and positive training methods are very effective.

These characteristics enable the Poodle to be a highly versatile dog, capable of learning many different skills. As entertainers, Poodles are credited with performing unusual and challenging tricks to astound their audiences, and they make great partners for dog owners interested in participating in a number of canine sports, like flyball, agility, and obedience trials. Possessing a quick wit and an uncanny ability to reason, Poodles have amazed their owners throughout the ages with their inventive games and problem solving.

Because of his high level of intelligence, the Poodle is easy to train.

Considering their physical and temperamental qualities, it is obvious why so many people have become Poodle lovers. Their ideal size, practically shedless coat, devotion to their owners, and winning personalities make them a wonderful choice of pets. They are easy to keep, and they are suitable for just about any living accommodations. It is no wonder they have become one of the most popular dogs in the world!

PREPARING

for Your Toy or Miniature Poodle

Now that you have decided the Toy or Miniature Poodle is definitely the breed to fit your wants and lifestyle, you may be surprised to realize that there are still more decisions to make and more research to do! Searching for the dog of your dreams can be a demanding endeavor once it becomes obvious that not all Poodles are created equal. But with enough effort and careful consideration of your choices, you can feel confident that you are getting just the right canine companion for you.

PRELIMINARY DECISIONS

Puppy or Adult

There are advantages and disadvantages to getting either a puppy or an adult. You should absolutely consider these differences before making a definite choice!

Puppies are certainly more in demand, mainly because they are so irresistibly cute. Poodle pups are comical little balls of fluff, endearing and entertaining. Obtaining and raising a puppy can be a very rewarding experience, and it is fun to watch a puppy grow and mature into an adult dog. Best of all, you will have complete control over his training, environment, and experiences so that he will hopefully become a well-mannered, well-adjusted pet.

On the other hand, puppies are a lot of work and require a lot of time. You must supervise them constantly, and they should not be left alone for long periods. Housetraining entails vigilant observation, and of course, a lot of patience and carpet cleaner. Curious and often fearless, puppies have not yet learned household rules and must be taught to respect limits. Puppy owners must be on guard for potentially dangerous situations, such as exposed electrical cords that may become chewing targets or items that could become choking hazards. Puppies must be fed more often and given frequent potty breaks. They also will require a number of trips to the veterinarian for checkups and vaccinations. People who are not prepared for the energy level, destructiveness, expense, and time commitment of puppy ownership may find themselves overwhelmed.

In addition, puppies can be expensive. Add to the purchase price of the puppy the cost of altering, a series of puppy vaccinations, microchipping, registration fees, and the replacement of collars, beds, or dog crates that are eventually outgrown. There are also the underlying costs of replacing items the puppy may damage.

You may avoid some of these costs if you purchase an adult dog. An adult dog may already be altered, vaccinated, and housetrained. He will have outgrown the teething stage, during which most chewing occurs, and he may have had some training. But some expenses apply to both puppies and adult dogs. Grooming, for example, is an essential and important maintenance expense for Poodles of any age. The cost of pet supplies and obedience classes will apply to both puppies and adults as well and should be taken into consideration before getting any dog.

One of the advantages to purchasing an adult dog is that his personality is already established.

Another advantage to getting an adult is that adult dogs generally do not take as long to train. While a puppy has the short attention span and limited retention of a child, an adult dog does not require as much repetition in the process of learning. However, the possibility always exists that an adult dog will have some baggage in the form of bad habits that need correction. Without having the opportunity to raise the dog from puppyhood, some behavior issues may have developed, outside of your control, that will require some time and effort to resolve. Dog owners should be prepared to seek appropriate help and put forth the effort to solve any pre-existing problems.

Probably the greatest benefit in getting an adult dog is that *what you see is what you get*. If the dog has any existing behavior issues, they will immediately present themselves. Physical and temperamental traits have already established themselves, so you do not need to guess exactly how big, energetic, aggressive, friendly, dominant, submissive, dependent, or independent the dog will grow to be. This is different from puppies, who are merely potentials. You hope that a puppy will grow to become the kind of Toy or Miniature Poodle you have dreamed of owning, but there are no guarantees. Even the Puppy Aptitude Test (PAT) is limited in predicting how a puppy will turn out as an adult. Although the PAT is useful in determining which puppies will tend toward behavior or personality extremes, the environment in which the puppy has been raised has a lot of influence on the actual outcome. Puppies, after all, are not only a product of genetics; they are also a product of their environment. Early experiences in life may contribute to the development of fearfulness, aggression, or other undesirable traits.

When deciding whether to get a puppy or adult, dog buyers should consider their current lifestyles. A person who is too busy to invest the necessary time into raising a puppy should

The PAT and CPP

The Puppy Aptitude Test (PAT) is a method of evaluating a puppy's personality traits. Developed by renowned professional dog trainers Jack and Wendy Volhard, it has become the most widely used method for choosing a puppy. The method involves conducting a number of activities designed to evaluate confidence, dependence, dominance, and other personality traits, in addition to testing a puppy's structural soundness and sensitivities. It is a valuable tool in determining a puppy's suitability for various activities.

The Volhards have also developed a Canine Personality Profile (CPP) for adult dogs. This can help a dog owner understand her dog's personality and provide useful information for planning training strategies.

Both the PAT and CPP evaluations can be found in their entirety on the Volhards' website at www.volhard.com.

opt for an adult. This includes people who have demanding jobs or who are already trying to keep up with active children. For someone who has other pets, however, a puppy may be a good choice, because he will have the opportunity to interact with the other animal members of the household.

Male or Female

If you plan to show or breed your dog, you should consider some of the differences between the sexes. Male dogs who are not castrated may engage in undesirable, hormone-related behavior such as wandering, marking (urinating on furniture), and mounting just about anything that makes a good target (including the legs of your guests). These behaviors are normal for an unaltered male, but they can be annoying and embarrassing for a dog owner. Temperamentally, male dogs can become more dominant and aggressive. They are more prone to getting into fights with other male dogs and may become aggressive toward children, especially as they mature.

Unspayed females will go into heat twice a year and emit a bloody discharge to attract male suitors. Each heat cycle will last about three weeks, during which time the female may act anxious or flirty and attempt to wander in search of a mate. It can be a messy, stressful time for dog owners, and they must highly supervise the female to prevent accidental breeding.

If you are getting a dog as a pet, you should plan to have him or her altered. Castrating or spaying eliminates the undesirable behaviors associated with unaltered dogs. The procedures also prevent certain health conditions, such as tumors of the reproductive organs, false pregnancies, and perineal hernias. When altered, both sexes can make excellent pets, and choosing a sex then becomes a strictly personal choice. While some claim one sex or the other is more affectionate or easier to train, these traits are actually individual in nature and not gender specific.

A few noticeable differences are apparent between the sexes, regardless of whether or not sterilization has been performed. Physically, males may grow to be slightly larger than females. Due to their different physiologies, spaying a female is more complicated and expensive. Also, a male or female's method of elimination is necessarily different. However, these differences should not be cause to eliminate a pet prospect who otherwise meets your expectations and has an outstanding temperament.

Colors

Poodles come in a great variety of colors that provides interesting choices for buyers. While color may be a personal choice, the differences among colors may be more than skin deep. A breeder survey revealed that Poodles of different colors

Black Poodles have been found to be the most trainable and obedient.

exhibited slightly different behaviors, perhaps due to the breeding lines used to perpetuate a particular color.

Black and white Poodles are the most common and easiest to find. Regarding trainability and obedience, the black Poodle rated the highest, while the white Poodle placed a close second. These colors were also found to be less destructive, less wary of strangers, and more social with other dogs than some of the other Poodle colors.

Color differences also result in slightly different coats. The apricot Poodle's coat curls more easily, and so it is more difficult to achieve the straight, fluffy look required in a show ring.

Differences in temperament and coat type have proven to be relatively minor in range, but they do give a Poodle buyer something to think about.

WHERE TO FIND THE RIGHT DOG

The trick to finding the right dog is to shop around and keep specific goals in mind. This is no easy task, since almost all Poodles are adorable and difficult to resist. However, controlling the impulse to take home the first charming bundle of fur that captures your heart may save you much heartache later. Holding out for just the right dog is never a mistake. Even when it seems you may have passed up a good opportunity, another good opportunity always awaits.

Try making a list of the qualities you most desire in a dog. Maybe you want a Poodle who falls on the lower end of the activity level scale. Maybe you're partial to a particular color, sex, age, or size. (Some variation exists within the Miniature and Toy size classifications.) Keep these qualities in mind while searching for the perfect dog, because when you know exactly what you want, chances are you will not be disappointed with what you get.

Professional Breeders

Professional breeders are a good source of puppies and adult dogs. In addition to the puppies they raise, professional breeders will often assist in rehoming an adult dog when the owner can no longer keep him.

How to Find a Professional Breeder

Many people who show dogs also breed them, so dog shows are a good place to meet Poodle breeders and see some of their dogs. National and local Poodle clubs can provide information on Toy and Miniature Poodle breeders in your area, and you can also check with veterinarians or search the Internet to locate them.

Show- and Pet-Quality Poodles

If you are interested in showing and breeding your Poodle, a professional breeder is the only source you should consider. If you are new to the sport, you should seek advice and guidance from those more experienced, especially when choosing a show-quality puppy. Keep in mind that this activity involves considerable time and financial commitments, but it can provide many rewards as well.

If you simply want a Poodle for companionship, professional breeders are also a good source of pet-quality dogs. Almost

Choose a breeder whose dogs appear happy and healthy.

every litter of puppies includes a few individuals who do not meet the criteria of a show prospect—that is, some physical trait exists that deviates slightly from the breed standard. This trait may be as minor as eyes that are a bit too round or a coat color that has too much shading variation. Imperceptible to lay people, these traits may make a dog ineligible to participate in dog shows, but they do not affect his health or his potential to be a wonderful pet.

Is My Breeder Reputable?

A breeder can be an excellent source of quality dogs, whether you are looking for a show prospect or a pet, but it's important to know how to distinguish between those who are reputable and those who are not.

- **A reputable breeder concerns herself with producing the best possible specimens of a breed.** This involves selective breeding for the purpose of meeting the standards of a breed, attempting to produce the best temperaments possible, and breeding dogs who are free of inheritable health conditions.

- **Serious breeders will not breed dogs known to have genetic defects.** They may have tests performed regularly on their breeding stock, and if they have done this, they should provide documentation to prospective buyers. They may also require buyers to notify them if any of the puppies develop hereditary problems so that they can attempt to eliminate the problem from their breeding lines.

- **Conscientious breeders understand the importance of early socialization for puppies and will not sell puppies younger than eight weeks old.** Removing a puppy from his mother and littermates prior to this time deprives him of the opportunity to learn valuable social skills, which can cause behavioral or emotional problems later. At eight weeks old, the puppies should have already received at least one set of vaccinations and a worming treatment. Documentation of vaccinations should be available and should include type, manufacturer, serial number, and inoculation dates. Selling puppies younger than eight weeks old or puppies lacking age-appropriate vaccinations is a red flag—buyers beware!

- **Breeders who care about the health of their puppies provide a clean, safe environment in which the puppies can thrive.** Puppies who are dirty, smelly, or kept in

unsanitary conditions are prone to health problems. Avoid breeders who are not meticulous about their puppies' living conditions.

If you have determined that your prospective breeder is reputable, you should ask to see the parent dogs, if they are available. This will give you an indication of the physical characteristics and temperament the puppies will inherit. Remember, puppies do not remain puppies very long, so it's nice to know what to expect as they get older.

Paperwork

Breeders who are serious about producing quality dogs will register their dogs with a well-known and well-respected registry and will have detailed pedigree records available for the puppies. A pedigree will show the dog's family tree and will indicate if any inbreeding has occurred, which can increase a dog's chance of inheriting genetic defects. Those who breed unregistered dogs and do not keep pedigree records are not concerned with the quality of the puppies they produce.

Reputable breeders are also very concerned about who purchases their puppies. They will require buyers to sign a purchase contract that may include provisions requiring the buyer to alter the puppy or return the dog to the breeder if the owner can no longer keep him. A purchase contract will also spell out any health guarantees or requirements, a very valuable feature for puppy buyers.

After you have decided on a puppy, you will receive a sales contract, which you should review thoroughly. No standard puppy sales contract exists, so the requirements and guarantees can vary considerably from one contract to another. Be sure you understand all the provisions before signing the contract, and ask questions if anything is unclear. Most important, make sure that the contract is agreeable to you. Some contracts have very limited health guarantees, and others may place unreasonable burdens on the buyer.

Hobby Breeders

Hobby breeders are also referred to as "backyard breeders," and they are most often located through local ads, flyers, road signs, word-of-mouth, or veterinarians. They are private dog owners who happen to own one or more purebred dogs they have bred. The quality of the dogs produced may be questionable, since the hobby breeder may not be as familiar with breed standards as a serious breeder. Also, they may not have the knowledge of genetics to produce the best specimens of the breed, and they may not have the experience or the facilities to raise the puppies properly.

Some hobby breeders, however, produce good pet-quality dogs, and some of the methods for distinguishing between good hobby breeders and those you should avoid are the same as apply to professional breeders. If the hobby breeder breeds AKC-registered dogs, has tested the parent dogs for genetic defects, and has provided age-appropriate puppy vaccinations and clean living arrangements, you can be fairly certain that she is reputable.

Hobby breeders might not use puppy sales contracts or provide the health guarantees of a professional breeder, but they can be a good source of affordable purebred dogs. When purchasing a dog from any breeder, it helps to see the parent dogs and evaluate them for physical and temperamental traits. The sire may not be available if the hobby breeder contracted stud service from another breeder, but the dam should always

Reputable breeders will socialize their puppies from a young age.

be available for inspection. If the dam is not available, the breeder may actually be a broker (an intermediary who sells puppies for other breeders or puppy mills). It is best to avoid purchasing a puppy in this situation.

Animal Shelters

The animal shelter is one source of dogs often overlooked by those seeking a specific breed, such as a Toy or Miniature Poodle. Many people do not realize that up to 25 percent of the dogs taken into shelters are purebreds, the majority of whom are adults. The greatest fear people have about adopting a shelter dog is that of inheriting someone else's problem dog. The truth is that dogs are surrendered to shelters for many reasons. Sometimes the owner can no longer keep the dog due to circumstances beyond her control. Sometimes an owner dies. And sometimes an owner simply realizes she has chosen the wrong dog for her lifestyle. Shelters also take in stray and abused animals who are there through no fault of their own.

At the same time, some dogs in shelters will have serious behavior problems, but many treasures are also to be found there.

Cost

Getting a dog from a shelter has a number of advantages, the most obvious of which is the cost. Adoption fees are generally less than the price of a Poodle from any other source. Most shelters will have adult dogs altered and up-to-date on vaccinations before releasing them to a new home, thus eliminating many of the health care costs associated with getting a new dog. Shelter dogs are often temperament tested to

Petfinder.com

An excellent Internet resource for those wishing to adopt a Poodle can be found at www.petfinder.com. This national database of shelter dogs can help you locate specific breeds within a particular geographic area.

facilitate their placement in the right homes, and this can be used to your advantage to get a dog with the personality traits you desire. Animal shelters also provide services and support in the form of free advice, reduced-fee obedience classes, and informative seminars to help new dog owners get off to a good start.

Availability

The biggest problem faced in trying to locate a Poodle from an animal shelter is availability. If no Poodles are available for adoption, some shelters are willing to put prospective owners on a call list to notify them when the desired breed is available. Sometimes this entails a long wait, and sometimes not. (The turnover rate at animal shelters is rapid.) If the dog of your dreams is not available, check back a week later.

Paperwork

Although registration papers may not be available, this should not be an obstacle for those who simply desire a pet-quality Poodle. Nevertheless, it is important to accept the fact that shelter dogs often have a vague history and come with no health guarantees.

Animal shelters will require adopters to sign an adoption contract similar to a breeder's puppy-sale contract. It may require you to return the dog to them if you can no longer keep him. It may also specify the living arrangements you must provide for the dog. Most shelter adoption contracts are reasonable and do not cause undue hardship for adopters, since most of the provisions exist for the sole purpose of protecting the animal's welfare. It is still a good idea to review any contract thoroughly before signing.

Breed Rescues

Like animal shelters, breed rescues take in unwanted, abused, and stray dogs. Because they specialize in a particular breed, they are an excellent source for those looking for a purebred dog. Poodle rescue organizations have experience with the unique needs of the breed and are a good source of information, advice, and referrals. You can locate

Poodle rescue organizations by contacting breed registries such as the AKC, Poodle clubs, local animal shelters, or doing an Internet search.

These dogs, like shelter dogs, may not be registered or come with health guarantees. They may have pre-existing health or behavior issues, but just as likely, they may be good dogs that simply lack a home. Breed rescues usually do thorough evaluations on their dogs and can advise you if a dog is available as a good match for your needs, wants, and lifestyle.

Cost

Adoption fees and contracts for breed rescues are also similar to that of animal shelters. Although some breed rescues maintain kennels and operations similar to animal shelters, others are smaller, more loosely organized groups that provide foster homes for dogs in need until they can go to permanent homes.

Paperwork

Breed rescues are very concerned about matching dogs with the right owners. You will be required to fill out an application so that they can evaluate the suitability of your home for the particular dog you wish to adopt. Once your

application is approved, you will be required to sign an adoption contract that may specify the type of living accommodations you must provide, what kind of regular veterinary care is expected, and what must be done if you can no longer keep the dog. The exact contract requirements can vary considerably from one breed rescue to another, so it is in your best interest to review the contract thoroughly, and

Many rescued Poodles make great pets.

make sure that you understand all the provisions prior to signing.

Internet Sources

Technology has provided new options in the purchase of purebred dogs, that being the ability to locate and purchase puppies or dogs online. Breeders and hobby breeders in particular may offer the opportunity to purchase dogs via the Internet and deliver them or ship them directly to you. This method of selling and delivering dogs has its own advantages and disadvantages.

It has never been easier to locate the exact type of dog you desire. Regardless of your preferences, you can find precisely what you want anywhere in the country—or the world! Doing business online can be easy and efficient, and it provides more options than may be available locally. Nevertheless, some disadvantages must be considered. Buying a puppy isn't quite as simple as filling out an online order form. Evaluating the puppy or his parents in person is usually not practical or possible. Shipping a dog or puppy long distances can be stressful or traumatic for the animal, especially if he encounters delivery delays. In addition, if any sales contract disputes arise, they usually have to be settled in a court of law located within the breeder's state of residence. This can cause significant problems for the buyer, who may reside in a state across the country.

Internet use has some practical applications, however. Locating breeders, animal shelters, and breed rescues statewide and within surrounding states can expand the available pool of dogs from which to choose. Contacting and communicating with these sources online is easy and inexpensive. For those who are willing to travel in this wider area to inspect a prospect personally, there is a greater chance they will be able to locate just the right dog.

Pet Stores

Some people decide to buy a Toy or Miniature Poodle from a pet store. Pet stores can be a convenient option, and they usually offer a wide selection of puppies. It is important to remember, though, that a dog's health, happiness, and well-being are largely dependent on his genetics and the quality of his early care. This is why you must ask the pet store to provide you with all the details of the Toy or Mini Poodle's breeding and history. In fact, pet store employees should be knowledgeable about dogs in general and the breeds they sell in particular.

If you are considering a Poodle from a pet store, check the dog for any signs of poor health. A few signs of illness are nasal discharge, watery eyes, and diarrhea. A store should not be selling a dog experiencing any of these symptoms. Even if the puppy seems healthy, be sure to have him checked by your veterinarian as soon as possible. Many health guarantees offered by pet stores are contingent upon a veterinary examination within a few days of the sale.

Questions to Ask Before Purchasing a Pet-Store Puppy

You should ask some of the following questions of pet store personnel before committing to a sale:

1. **What kind of guarantee do you offer?**

   If the store only guarantees the puppy for a few hours or days but offers no compensation for future problems such as genetic diseases, you must be aware that you will be on your own to deal with these problems. The store should be reasonably responsible for ensuring that you receive a healthy puppy.

2. **How old was the puppy when he arrived in the store?**

   Puppies taken away from their mother and littermates before eight weeks of age are at a great developmental disadvantage. Puppies learn a lot about social interaction from their mother and littermates, and getting shipped across the country in a crate is no way to begin life as a six-week-old puppy. Those taken away too young and exposed to these frightening experiences often develop fearful or aggressive behaviors later in life. The best-case scenario is one in which the puppy was hand delivered by a breeder to a pet store after eight weeks of age.

3. **Can I see the vaccination and worming record?**

   Puppies should have had at

least one and preferably two sets of complete vaccinations and a worming by eight weeks. (This can also depend on the breed.) The pet store should have complete documentation of these and any other veterinary care the dogs have received.

4. Is the puppy registered?

Registration is no guarantee of quality, and some registries will register any dog without proof of a pedigree (a written record of a dog's lineage). Dogs who are registered with the American Kennel Club or Kennel Club may be more likely to come from breeders who are following certain standards, but it's not a guarantee. However, the AKC does at least have minimum standards for record keeping and care for large breeders.

Some small local breeders may provide to pet stores puppies who are unregistered but who could make healthy, fine pets. Ask about this, because it will help get the employees talking about the dog and the breeder. The more questions you ask about the store's source of puppies, the more you might be able to find out about the breeder's priorities and history.

CHOOSING A PUPPY

Now that you know where to find Toy and Miniature Poodles, you may face the task of deciding which one to take home. If you are choosing a puppy from a litter, this can be exceptionally difficult, because all puppies are cute, playful, and fun. Nevertheless, there are some things you can look for to narrow your choices.

The first thing you should check is the health of the puppies. Runny noses, squinty eyes, and lethargy are signs of ill health. A puppy should be robust, active, and alert. The coat should be thick and free of parasites and excess dander. If one sick puppy is present in a litter, the other puppies may also be ill, even if they do not show any symptoms.

Once determined to be healthy, you can evaluate the puppies for temperament and apply your personal preferences to find the right one. It is easy to let your heart be carried away with the first outgoing puppy who immediately claims you as his own. It is just as tempting to fall for the small, timid runt of the litter who seems to need your love and nurturing most of all. However, most experts suggest considering something in between—a puppy who thinks and evaluates a situation before acting but who is also outgoing and friendly. In other words, try to avoid puppies who display temperament extremes.

BEFORE YOUR PUPPY COMES HOME

It is easy to become caught up in the excitement of getting a new Poodle puppy and forget how much work must be done preparing to bring him home. This is why it is a good idea to do some of the preparation in advance, rather than wait until the puppy has already arrived.

Obtain Supplies

You can obtain some of the supplies you need ahead of time and save yourself the frustration of rushing at the last minute, trying to locate everything. Even if you are not exactly sure what size bed or what brand of food to purchase, shopping

When choosing your Poodle puppy, look for one who is robust, active, and alert.

Pre-Puppy Prep

Here are some things you should do before your puppy comes home:

1. Obtain supplies

2. Puppy-proof your home

3. Set up sleeping and confinement arrangements

4. Establish household rules

around will let you know where to get what you need when you are ready for it.

Consider purchasing the following supplies for your new Toy or Miniature Poodle puppy.

Collar

Measure your dog's neck prior to shopping for a collar so that you can purchase the correct size. Puppies will require an adjustable collar that can be enlarged as they grow.

Leash

A 6-foot (1.8-m) leash is the best for dog walks or training. Keep your dog's size in mind when choosing a leash. Toy and Miniature Poodles do not require a thick or heavy-duty form of restraint. A light, flexible nylon web leash is sufficient.

Identification

The following methods of identification will help your dog find his way home in the event that he is lost or stolen:

- **Identification tags** are a good first line of defense in preventing loss or theft, because they provide an immediate form of identification. Your neighbors are unlikely to own microchip scanners, so if they discover your wandering dog, identification tags will provide an instantly recognizable form of identification.

- **Microchipping** is a method of identification that involves injecting a small, rice-sized computer chip under the skin between the dog's shoulders. This is a relatively painless procedure, similar to a vaccination, that your veterinarian can perform. The dog's owner can then be identified when a scanner is held over the dog to read the information on the computer chip. The advantage of microchipping is that it is a permanent form of identification that cannot be lost or removed from the dog. A disadvantage is that, because several manufacturers produce microchips, scanners are not capable of reading all the microchips on the market. Negotiations are currently underway among manufacturers to standardize these products and eliminate this problem.

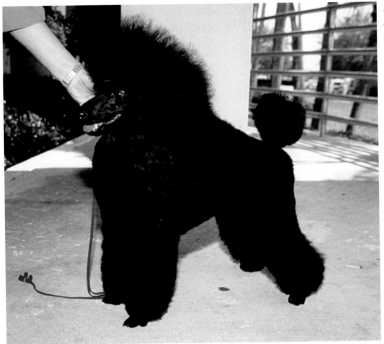

A light, flexible leash is sufficient for Toy and Miniature Poodles.

Even so, microchipping remains one of the best permanent forms of identification available.

- **Tattoos** are another permanent form of identification. Dogs can be tattooed, usually on the belly, underside of the ear, or inside of the back leg, with numbers or letters that can identify the dog. This has become a less popular alternative with the advent of microchips, but it is still a valid option. The disadvantage of tattooing is that hair may grow over the tattoo, making it difficult to locate or read. Tattoos also can be altered or may blur with age. On the positive side, it is the only visible form of permanent identification available.

  Participating veterinarians or authorized agents can perform tattooing, which is a relatively painless procedure. The tattoo should be registered with a national organization such as the National Dog Registry or Tattoo-A-Pet. If you decide to have your dog tattooed, be sure to use information that will not change in the future. A social security number can always be traced back to you, while an address or phone number may change.

  Finally, don't forget to obtain your dog's license, as required by most communities. In addition to providing identification for your dog, licensing encourages compliance with rabies vaccination laws. If you fail to license your dog, you may face fines and other expenses.

Identification tags will help your Poodle find his way home should he become lost.

Food and Water Bowls

Stainless steel bowls between 8 (0.23 kg) and 16 ounces (0.45 kg) in size will suffice for Toy Poodles, and 10- (0.28 kg) to 20-ounce (0.57 kg) bowls are a good size for Miniatures.

Food and Water

Initially, try to purchase the brand of food your dog received before he came home with you. It doesn't hurt to have some bottled water on hand in case your tap water smells or tastes differently from what your dog is used to.

Crate

The crate should be large enough for your dog to stand, turn around, and lay down in comfortably, but it should not have a lot of excess space. For puppies, you may need to purchase a larger crate as your puppy grows.

Doggy Bed

Toy Poodles will feel cozy in a small bed approximately 20 (50.8 cm) to 24 inches (61.0 cm) wide, and Miniatures nestle nicely in a small- to medium-sized bed approximately 22 (55.9 cm) to 28 inches (71.1 cm) wide.

Grooming Tools

The minimum grooming tools necessary for general Toy and Miniature Poodle maintenance include a small slicker brush, medium-toothed comb, straight shears, and small- or medium-size nail clippers.

Boundary Spray

Sprays intended for both indoor and outdoor use are the most versatile. They can help solve a number of behavior issues that inevitably crop up when you bring a new dog or puppy into your home.

Pooper-Scooper

Pooper-scoopers with long handles can save you a lot of back strain when cleaning up after your dog, but dog-doo bags are another option that is less expensive, convenient, and just as efficient for cleaning up after small dogs like Toy and Miniature Poodles.

Toys and Treats

Offer your dog a variety of toys that provide different textures and hardness so that he can choose his favorites. Toy and Miniature Poodles favor small, soft, chewy treats that are easy for their tiny mouths to handle.

Puppy-Proof Your Home

Take a moment to check your home for potential safety problems. Puppies are as curious and ignorant of danger as young children. Make exposed electrical cords, poisonous household plants, and dangerous household products inaccessible. Also, take care to keep the floor clear of chewable items, like shoes and children's toys.

Your Poodle's crate serves as a safe haven, and it facilitates the housetraining process.

Set Up Sleeping and Confinement Arrangements

Establishing sleeping and confinement arrangements in advance will alert you to any objections from family members and give you some time to puppy-proof a confinement area. It is just as important to determine where the dog will be taken for potty breaks, because using the same outdoor area will assist with housetraining.

Establish Household Rules

If children reside in the home, you must establish household rules. Is there any place in the home the puppy will not be allowed? Who will be responsible for feeding and caring for the puppy? Who will clean up after him? Brief children on how to handle and play with a puppy correctly before his arrival, and consider what limits might need to be placed on playtime.

AFTER YOUR PUPPY COMES HOME

Bringing your new Toy or Miniature Poodle home is a very exciting event. However, it is important to keep a few key things

Offer your Poodle a variety of toys that provide different textures and hardness.

in mind in order to make his transition to your home as smooth as possible.

Limit Puppy's Activity

Keep your puppy's first few days at home as quiet as possible. The stress and overstimulation of adjusting to a new environment can result in stomach upset, exhaustion, and illness. It helps to limit activity with children and other pets, and you should provide a quiet, comfortable retreat where the puppy can escape from all the excitement. Providing plenty of toys will give the puppy opportunities to relieve stress in appropriate ways, and frequent outdoor breaks will supply fresh air and get him started on the right track for housetraining.

Introduce Other Pets Slowly

If you already have other pets at home, introduce them to your new canine friend slowly. Keeping pets separated for the first few days will give them the chance to become accustomed to each other's scent and presence. This can be accomplished with door gates or other methods of restraint or confinement. The first physical meeting should be conducted with the puppy and any other dogs on leashes so that you can intervene immediately if any problems develop.

When properly introduced and given enough time to adjust to each other, most pets can adapt to living in the same household. Even in cases in which your pets do not become bonded as best buddies, they can learn to tolerate each other and live together peacefully.

Bond With Your Puppy

If possible, don't leave the puppy alone for long periods during the first week. Bringing the puppy home before a long weekend or while you're on vacation will give you the opportunity to spend some time with your new family member so that you can get to know each other. This is an important bonding time for you and your new dog. It will also afford you the time to make the necessary initial veterinary appointment, which should be done within the first few days of your puppy's arrival.

Take Puppy to the Vet

Even if your puppy is already up to date on vaccinations, a veterinary check will detect any health conditions that may have escaped your untrained eye. If you are party to a puppy sales contract, a vet check will be required to validate any health guarantees. In either case, this is also a good time to ask your veterinarian any questions you may have about the puppy's health, care, or development, and to have your puppy microchipped if this has not already been performed.

TRAVELING WITH YOUR DOG

Toy and Miniature Poodles make excellent traveling companions. They enjoy spending time with their owners immensely, and they are always more than happy to join you on trips or vacations. Their small size and nearly shedless coats make them welcome guests at many lodgings, and you can transport them easily in a travel crate or bag when embarking on various modes of transportation.

When properly introduced, most pets can adapt to living in the same household.

Before Your Trip

Before traveling with your Toy or Miniature Poodle, you should adhere to the following:

1. **Make sure your dog is healthy and up to date on vaccinations.** For extended trips or international travel, you should have your dog examined by a veterinarian and obtain a certificate of health. When planning to enter a foreign country, check the health requirements and quarantine procedures of your

destination, and have the necessary paperwork prepared.

2. **Familiarize your dog with the mode of travel.** If you plan to travel by car, make sure your dog is comfortable riding in a vehicle and being restricted or confined by a traveling crate or doggy seat belt. Taking him on short trips around town will help prepare your dog for car travel. Dogs who become carsick or overly nervous can be desensitized to car travel, or in the case of extreme sickness or anxiety, may benefit from medications prescribed by your veterinarian. When traveling by plane or cruise ship, you will be required to transport your dog in a travel crate or bag, so give him plenty of opportunities to become accustomed to his crate or bag ahead of time.

3. **Check the requirements and restrictions of commercial modes of travel.** Buses, trains, and smaller cruise ships rarely allow passengers to transport pets aboard. Planes and larger cruise ships may allow pets, but they often have specific requirements for the size and type of travel crate, labeling requirements, and health documentation.

4. **Locate dog-friendly lodging in advance.** Nothing is more frustrating than reaching your destination to find that most of the hotels and motels in the area do not allow pets. Your travel agent or Internet sources can help you locate appropriate lodging prior to your departure.

5. **Pack your dog's necessary care items.** Bring a supply of your dog's regular food to last a little longer than your trip;

Finding the Lost Dog

If you discover that your dog is lost, follow the steps listed below to increase your chances of finding your pet as quickly as possible:

1. Walk the neighborhood and talk to neighbors. Call your dog while doing so. If your dog responds to a special word like "treat" or has a favorite squeaky toy, use these as enticements. Leave a description of your pet and your phone number with neighbors. Neighborhood children often make an enthusiastic search team, but instruct them not to call the dog unless the dog is in sight. Having a lot of strange people calling a dog's name at once can be confusing and frightening for a lost dog.

2. Call local shelters, Poodle rescue groups, and government agencies responsible for animal control. Most shelters are only required to hold lost pets for 72 hours before placing them for adoption, so you should contact them at least every other day. Include all shelters and agencies within a 20-mile radius.

3. Make flyers with photos and a description of your dog to distribute to veterinarians, groomers, trainers, and pet stores. You can also post flyers anywhere public bulletin boards are located, such as banks or grocery stores. Because a Poodle's appearance changes with the growth of his hair, use photos that most closely represent how your dog looked when he disappeared. To avoid scam artists, do not include your name or address on the flyers. You can include your phone number and reward information if desired.

4. Place an ad in local newspapers. Some newspapers are willing to publish lost pet ads for free. Also, check the found ads frequently. Always withhold some piece of identifying information so that you can qualify the leads you receive.

Travel Care Items

The following supplies will come in handy the next time you are traveling with your Poodle:

- Food
- Local or bottled water
- Collar
- Identification tags
- Leash
- Brush and comb
- Treats
- Pooper-scooper
- Medications
- First-aid kit for dogs

you never know if your return may be delayed for a day or two. Bring a sufficient amount of local or bottled water, because some dogs may refuse to drink regional water that tastes or smells differently. Other necessary items include your dog's collar and identification tags, leash, brush and comb (campers beware—Poodles attract burdocks and other plant matter), treats, pooper-scooper, medications, and doggy first-aid kit (especially for campers). Be sure to bring some doggy toys to provide diversion and stress relief. A few long-lasting chews or a treat-holding toy may help keep your dog busy and reduce barking if you need to leave him alone for short periods. It is also a good idea to bring a photo of your dog, along with vital information, in case your dog becomes lost. You should keep your veterinarian's number on hand for emergencies.

6. **Feed your dog a light meal and give him an opportunity to relieve himself before you leave.** You may have to withhold food prior to traveling if your dog is prone to motion sickness.

During Your Trip

While traveling with your Toy or Miniature Poodle, the following are some suggestions to ensure the safety of your pet:

1. Make sure your dog receives breaks to relieve himself and stretch his legs occasionally. Offer him plenty of drinking water during your trip.
2. Never leave your dog unattended in a closed vehicle while traveling, especially in warmer climates. If you must leave your dog in the car for a short period of time, make sure there is plenty of ventilation. Keeping the vehicle windows open and using a battery-operated crate fan that can be attached to his crate or the car window will aid air circulation.
3. Do not let your dog travel with his head out the window, because this can cause eye and ear injuries.
4. Be respectful of others. Clean up after your dog, prevent excessive barking, and keep your dog leashed. Responsible dog owners help to ensure that our pets will continue to be welcome at our favorite vacation spots.

If Your Dog Can't Join You

Sixty percent of American households have two incomes. This means that a lot of dogs are left home alone while their owners work, which can cause problems for both dogs and their owners. Dogs can suffer from boredom, a lack of exercise, and the stress of loneliness. Dog owners sometimes find themselves dealing with the destruction wrought by their lonely pet or find it difficult to provide adequate exercise and attention. In addition to that, demanding jobs often require dog owners to travel, work late, or work inconsistent shifts, making it hard to meet the needs of a pet. Fortunately, options are available that can help solve some of these problems and make it possible for people to keep a Toy or Miniature Poodle who otherwise wouldn't be able to own dogs.

Pet Sitters

In-home pet sitters are available to care for your dog in your own home, which allows your dog to remain in a familiar, nonstressful environment when you are gone. Their services may include midday dog walks to provide exercise and diversion during the day, visits to administer medications, and pet care during vacations.

In-home pet sitting is a great alternative to boarding your dog at a kennel while you are traveling or vacationing, because pet sitters can provide house-sitting services as well. They will bring in your mail and newspapers, turn lights on and off, and open and close drapes so that potential burglars do not know you are away. They often water plants and provide grooming services as well.

You can find a pet sitter in your area through the telephone book, veterinarians, humane societies, dog trainers, neighbors, or friends. The National Association of Professional Pet Sitters (NAPPS) or Pet Sitters International (PSI) can provide referrals for pet sitters who are accredited through their organizations. But even accredited pet sitters should be screened to make sure they are insured, bonded, and experienced.

Make sure that the pet sitter is familiar with the unique needs of your dog, ask for references, and initiate a meeting to make sure that your dog and the pet sitter are comfortable with each other. The pet sitter should show a genuine interest in your dog and ask about his history, habits, and health. The services contracted should be documented, as should emergency contact information.

Doggy Day Care Centers

Doggy day care centers, once considered a luxury for spoiled pets, have become a popular resource for busy pet owners. Operating much like a child day care facility, dog owners drop their dogs off in the morning on their way to work and pick them up at the end of the workday. While at the day care center, dogs can receive group playtime with other dogs, rest time, and snacks.

Doggy day care centers can provide wonderful experiences for a dog, but they are not for everybody. Dogs must be screened to make sure their temperaments are suitable for group activities. Dogs who have a protective or aggressive nature will be declined, and dogs who are aged or overly shy may not do well in such an active and noisy environment. Health requirements also must be met, including proof of current vaccinations such as distemper, parvovirus, hepatitis, rabies, and bordetella. Some day care centers will not allow dogs who are not altered.

If your dog is a good candidate for doggy day care, you should scrutinize doggy day care centers with the same concern as when choosing a child-care center. The ratio of staff to dogs should not exceed 10 to 12 dogs for every staff member, and the dogs should be adequately supervised and separated if their play becomes too rough. The staff should be knowledgeable about dogs and show competency in handling them.

In-home pet sitters will care for your dog in your own home.

As smaller members of the canine family, Toy and Miniature Poodles should not be grouped with larger dogs whose rough play might injure them. You should be sure the doggy day care provides groups of smaller dogs for socialization. And because the Poodle is a sensitive creature, the stress of spending all day at a doggy day care facility may be too much for some Poodles to handle. If your dog shows signs of stress, such as stomach upset, diarrhea, or depression, he may not be suited for the day care environment.

Boarding Kennels

Many boarding kennels have updated their operations to meet the demands of modern pet owners and now offer doggy day care services and in-home pet sitting services as adjuncts to their business. Others have expanded their traditional kennel operations to include daily exercise or group social activities, much to the benefit of their canine charges.

When evaluating a boarding kennel, cleanliness is paramount. Not only should the living areas be clean and uncluttered, but the dogs themselves should be clean and dry. Soft bedding should be available, and clean water should be provided at all times. Kennel staff should show an interest in their canine guests and be very knowledgeable in the care and treatment of dogs.

Preparing for the arrival of your new canine companion can take a lot of stress out of adjusting to this change in your life. With preparations complete, you and your new dog will have more time to enjoy each other's company and get off to a great start on your journey in life together!

The "New" Boarding Kennel

A number of newer boarding facilities have embraced the trend toward more comfortable lodgings for dogs by providing individual rooms instead of kennels, some complete with furniture and television sets. Although more expensive, these facilities attempt to alleviate a dog owner's anxiety about leaving her dogs in a strange place by creating a home-like atmosphere and customized care.

When evaluating a boarding kennel, make sure that the living areas are clean and uncluttered.

FEEDING
Your Toy or Miniature Poodle

D ogs, like any other type of animal, require a specialized diet to meet the unique nutritional needs of their species. However, breed-specific and individual dietary needs also must be considered. The health of your Toy or Miniature Poodle depends on feeding the type of food that is best for him. It also involves feeding the correct quantity at appropriate intervals and knowing how to avoid or correct feeding problems like obesity or finicky eating.

DIET OPTIONS

The food choices facing consumers these days are vast and diverse. While the array of products on the market does provide some advantages, it often causes just as much confusion. Dog food, like so many other products, comes in a variety of forms. Different brands, different life stage formulas, and various specialty diets are available. Home-cooked dog foods and raw diets are also options.

Choosing the right diet for a canine companion has become a matter of investigation and personal convenience. A discussion of the general types of dog foods may help you get started on narrowing your choices.

Commercial Foods

Prior to World War II, most dogs subsisted on table scraps and unusable portions of people food, much to the detriment of their health and teeth. Processed dog foods emerged as a method of using the by-products from human food processing, and although slightly better than table scraps and certainly rating higher on the convenience scale, the first prepackaged dog foods were lacking substantially in nutrition. The production of prepackaged dog foods has since reached a more advanced level, and manufacturers produce foods appropriate for different growth stages, activity levels, and health conditions.

Types of Commercial Food

Prepackaged dog foods now come in three different forms: dry, which

Dry foods compose the most popular meal base for dogs.

consists of 6 to 10 percent moisture; moist, which contains 23 to 40 percent moisture; and canned food, which is loaded with 68 to 80 percent moisture. Dry food is available in kibble form, which has a long shelf life and is generally the least expensive type of food. Moist foods also have a relatively long shelf life and are more palatable and easier for some dogs to chew. Canned foods are the most palatable for dogs; however, due to their high water content, it takes a larger volume of food by weight to provide enough sustenance. Canned foods, therefore, are the most expensive to feed.

Finding a Good-Quality Commercial Food

Because moist foods contain more sugar and additives than dry foods, and canned foods are more expensive and tend to cause dental problems because they stick to the teeth, these forms of dog food are used most often as supplements to dry food rather than as staple diets. With dry foods composing the most popular meal base for dogs, it is important to evaluate them the most carefully. The quality of dry prepackaged foods can vary considerably, and price is not always a determinant of quality. The only way to assess the quality of a commercially prepared dry dog food is to read the label.

Consider the following things in your search for a good-quality dog food:

• **Choose a dog food with a high-quality protein source.** The first ingredient listed should be a specific meat product. Dog foods that describe meat products as "by-products" or "meal" use lower quality meat ingredients than those listing simply chicken, lamb, or beef. Dog food manufacturers sometimes use soy or grain products as a source of protein, but these ingredients are inferior to the real thing—meat. Foods that contain real meat products may be more expensive, but you will need to feed smaller amounts, thus making the actual price difference negligible.

- **Find out what kind of preservative has been used.** In line with the trend toward more natural dog foods, some manufacturers now use vitamin E or C as preservatives instead of artificial preservatives such as ethoxyquin, butylated hydroxytoluene (BHT), or butylated hydroxyanisole (BHA). The preservative ethoxyquin, in particular, has been suspected of causing a number of health problems in dogs. Because vitamins E and C are not as effective as artificial preservatives, food preserved with these natural ingredients should be consumed within four to six months of the date of manufacture.

- **Check the source of fatty acids.** Fatty acids contribute to a healthy skin and coat and also affect general health. Quality sources of this ingredient include fish meal, fish oil, and flaxseed oil. These are loaded with omega-3 and omega-6 fatty acids, which are especially good for dogs with skin irritations or allergies. A poor source of fatty acids is animal fat, which is obtained from unspecified animals in unspecified portions, making its quality questionable. Animal fat and beef tallow, both inferior ingredients, are also very low in linoleic acid, which is important for skin and coat health.

- **Make sure the product meets standards set by the Association of American Feed Control Officials (AAFCO).** If so, the package label will state "formulated to meet the AAFCO Dog Food Nutrient Profile," which means that the product conforms to minimum standards as a complete and balanced dog food. Keep in mind that these are *minimum* standards, and they do not distinguish between

Choose a dog food with a high-quality protein source.

good, better, and best dog foods.

- **Avoid generic or store brands**. These brands often contain cheaper, poorer quality ingredients. Some generic brands are pet foods rejected by larger manufacturers and repackaged for sale under a generic label.

Varieties of Commercial Food

Once you have decided on a brand of dog food that meets your expectations for quality ingredients, you will face a variety of different forms of the product. Performance, super-premium, premium, maintenance, and economy versions of many dog foods are available. What distinguishes these different types are the protein and fat levels, which are located in the guaranteed analysis chart on the dog food label.

- **Performance dog foods** have exceptionally high crude protein and crude fat levels—up to 32 percent crude protein and 20 percent crude fat—and do not contain soy. (Remember, soy is a poorer source of protein than meat.) This type of food is designed for dogs who utilize a considerable amount of calories, and unless your dog is in training to enter the next Iditarod race, this is not an appropriate food for most dogs.

What Is the "Crude" in Protein and Fat?

"Crude" refers to the total protein and fat content levels in a dog food, regardless of how much of the protein and fat is actually digestible. Nondigestible proteins and fats are not utilized by the body and are expelled. Thus, the crude protein and crude fat percentages shown on the guaranteed analysis charts on dog food labels are rough guidelines as to the actual amount of protein and fat in the food. The actual amount of usable protein and fat is determined by the quality of the ingredients. Better sources of protein provide more usable protein for the body, and better sources of fat provide more usable fat.

- **Super-premium dog foods** contain, for the most part, approximately 23 to 27 percent crude protein and 12 to 16 percent crude fat. They also do not contain soy. This type of food is appropriate for working dogs and may be a good choice for dogs entering the show ring. The higher concentrations of protein and fat help contribute to a robust, healthy coat, but care must be taken to avoid weight gain for dogs who are not active enough to burn up the extra calories.

- **Premium dog foods** are adequate for the majority of dogs, with most of these foods falling between 21 to 25 percent crude protein and 10 to 14 percent crude fat. These products may or may not contain soy, so you must rely on the ingredient list to be sure that quality sources of protein are used. Some premium foods are adequate for light working dogs or show dogs. Pets who have advanced to quality premium foods will show a marked improvement in coat condition.

- **Maintenance diets** contain approximately 18 to 21 percent crude protein and 8 to 10 percent crude fat, and these foods often include soy products as a source of protein. Although a dog can certainly subsist on this type of diet, and it may even be a good choice for dogs who gain too much weight or have other problems with premium foods, do not expect your dog to attain the luxurious, shiny coat required of a show dog.

- **Economy foods** are a prime example that you get what you pay for. Low in crude protein, low in crude fat, and almost always containing soy products, economy foods meet the bare requirements of a complete and balanced dog food and usually contain substandard ingredients. This type of food is not recommended unless your budget absolutely cannot afford a better quality dog food.

Home-Cooked Foods

The problems and complexities of assessing the quality of commercially prepared dog foods have fueled a trend toward fresh food options. Commercial dog foods, like processed human foods, often contain unfamiliar ingredients, preservatives, and additives used to enhance color and flavor. In addition, product labels do not indicate the quality of the products used. For instance, a prepackaged food that shows chicken as the main ingredient won't specify if the chicken was rejected for human consumption due to poor quality or other reasons. For those interested in providing a healthier, more natural diet for their dog, home-cooked dog foods may be a desirable option.

Ingredients often include cooked meats, hard-boiled eggs, cottage cheese, cooked soybeans or lentils, cooked macaroni or rice, and cooked vegetables such as potatoes and pureed mixed vegetables. Probiotic and vitamin supplements round out the home-cooked menu to enhance digestion and nutrition. Meals can be made in bulk, enough to supply a week's worth of meals, and then stored in the refrigerator or freezer.

The greatest challenge in feeding home-cooked foods to your dog is creating balanced meals to meet your dog's nutritional requirements. It also involves sacrificing convenience and cost. Those who are serious about feeding this alternative to commercial

General Feeding Tips

Feed your dog at the same time(s) every day.

Switch to new foods gradually.

Provide fresh drinking water daily.

Keep your dog's water and food bowls clean.

Remove excess food after 30 minutes of feeding time.

Measure the amounts of food, monitor your dog's food intake, and watch for weight gain.

Feed pets separately so that you can monitor what each animal consumes.

Your Poodle should have access to plenty of fresh, cool water.

Raw Food (BARF) Diets

pet foods should research this option thoroughly and weigh the benefits and disadvantages.

One of the newest trends in dog food is to take natural foods a step further and feed them raw—a diet that proponents claim more closely resembles that which dogs would eat in the wild. Once considered a passing fad, its growth in popularity has assured its continued practice.

Supported by holistic sources as the most healthy, natural diet available, its value is based on the premise that cooked foods, whether prepared commercially or at home, lose valuable nutrients during the heating process. Strong debate still exists whether BARF diets are beneficial or dangerous. On the side of benefits, proponents suggest it can boost a dog's immune system, slow the aging process, and reduce the chance of degenerative or genetic diseases. But the United States Food and Drug Administration (FDA) and some experts in the veterinary community warn of the dangers of parasites and bacteria harbored in raw meat, as well as the possibility of internal damage from the consumption of bones. It is difficult to ignore the testimonials of those who have tried it. It is just as hard to disregard the compelling advice of experts who warn us that raw meat does *not* resemble wild animal food, because it has been processed and lacks the organs and other tissues that are consumed in the wild.

Raw diets can include a variety of protein sources, such as chicken wings or backs, raw eggs, hamburger, beef liver, or fish. Vegetable, cereal, and sometimes milk ingredients are added to make these diets nutritionally complete. These diets can also be supplemented with enzymes and vitamins. Due to the uncooked nature of the food, meals cannot be made more than a day in advance and are usually combined immediately before feeding.

Like home-cooked dog foods, dog owners must research this option thoroughly before attempting to feed this kind of diet. Ian Billinghurst's book, *Give Your Dog a Bone*, credited with popularizing the BARF diet, is a good resource on the subject.

Special Diets

Special diets are often a necessary component in the treatment of various health conditions. Dogs suffering from kidney, liver, heart, or urinary tract problems can benefit from commercially prepared specialty diets or home-prepared diets. Special diets can also help with diabetes, allergic skin reactions, or obesity. However, special diets should only be used on the recommendation of your veterinarian. The proper diagnosis of any health condition is necessary before deciding which special diet is appropriate to manage a condition.

Bones

Toy and Miniature Poodles are not heavy chewers, but puppies need to chew when teething, and adult dogs naturally clean their teeth by gnawing on hard objects. Bones may seem like the most obvious choice of chewing materials, but most veterinarians do not recommend them because they can splinter, become ingested, and cause internal problems. A better choice is synthetic or consumable dental chews or nylon bones, such as Nylabones, that are suitable in size for the smaller Poodle.

Treats

How boring our meals would be if we never had dessert! Dogs like something especially tasty to eat once in a while, too. Toy and Miniature Poodles prefer treats that are soft and easy to chew. Even if you opt for one of the all-natural, healthy treats now on the market, keep in mind that treats do not replace a healthy meal, and the consumption of any type of treats should be limited.

FEEDING FOR EVERY LIFE STAGE

From puppies to adults and from adults to seniors, dogs go through life stages that affect their nutritional needs. Adjusting your dog's diet to address the specific needs of each life stage will positively affect his health, longevity, and the quality of life he is able to enjoy.

Vitamins and Supplements

No single dog food is completely adequate for every dog at every life stage. In particular, puppies, pregnant or lactating females, aged dogs, or those with health conditions may require vitamins or supplements to meet their nutritional needs. Supplementing a dog's diet can also improve overall health and may be indicated if your dog displays a lackluster coat, dry skin, dull eyes, or a lack of energy.

Keep in mind that most dogs do just fine on a premium-quality commercial dog food. In the absence of physical signs indicating their use, supplements and vitamins are not generally necessary. However, they can provide dog owners with the peace of mind that their pet is receiving all his nutritional requirements. Consult with your veterinarian if you think your dog may benefit from vitamins or supplements.

Feeding Your Puppy

If you know what brand and type of dog food your Poodle puppy received before you got him, it is best to keep him on the same diet until he has settled into the new routines of your household. Changing his dog food abruptly, combined with the stress of adapting to a new environment, is a sure prescription for stomach upset and diarrhea. While your puppy settles into his new home, you can use this time to research various dog foods before making the decision to change to the food of your choice.

If and when you are ready to change your puppy's diet, it should be done gradually. Start out by mixing a little of the new food into the old food. Gradually increase the portion of new food while decreasing the portion of old food over a period of one to two weeks, until the puppy transitions completely.

Toy and Miniature Poodle puppies should be fed a good-quality puppy food until they are at least eight months old. Puppies between 8 and 12 weeks old should be fed three times per day, and puppies over 12 weeks old can be reduced to twice-daily feedings. Although some experts suggest reducing feedings to once per day when a puppy approaches a year old, there are some advantages to maintaining two feedings per day throughout your dog's adulthood.

Give your Poodles treats that are soft and easy to chew.

Feeding once in the morning and once in the evening encourages regular, predictable bowel movements, reducing the chance of your dog having an accident in the house. For working families, a morning feeding can keep your dog satiated and comfortable during the day, while an evening feeding will help subdue the temptation to beg at the dinner table. Toy and Miniature Poodles, due to their smaller size and high activity level, tend to do well on twice-daily feedings. It is always better to feed smaller portions more frequently than to feed a large quantity all at once.

Determining the appropriate amount to feed depends on the size of the puppy. You should follow the manufacturer's recommendations on the puppy food package, measure the food accurately, and adjust the amount according to your own observations. If your puppy doesn't completely finish his meal within 20 to 30 minutes, you are feeding him too much. If he cleans his bowl within ten minutes, you might not be feeding him enough. Adjust the amount of food until your puppy eats all but a few pieces of kibble within his 20- to 30-minute feeding time, and then remove the excess food.

Leaving excess food for your puppy to snack on during the day encourages irregular eating habits and leads to inconsistent bowel movements. This can make housetraining a greater challenge. It can also result in excessive weight gain, as the puppy will be consuming more food than he needs. You must be observant of your puppy's food intake throughout his puppyhood, because his increasing size and growth spurts may require you to adjust how much you feed him occasionally.

Sample Dry Food Feeding Schedule for Toy Poodles*

Age	Weight	Type of Food	Cups Per Day	Ounces
6–11 Weeks	2–3 lb (0.9–1.4 kg)	Puppy	$^1/_2$–1 (118.3–236.6 ml)	2–4 (0.06–0.11 kg)
3–4 Months	3–5 lb (1.4–2.3 kg)	Puppy	$^3/_4$–1$^1/_4$ (177.4–295.7 ml)	3–5 (0.09–0.14 kg)
5–7 Months	5–10 lb (2.3–4.5 kg)	Puppy	1–1$^1/_2$ (236.6–354.9 ml)	4–6 (0.11–0.17 kg)
8–12 Months	6–11 lb (2.7–5.0 kg)	Puppy	1$^1/_4$–1$^3/_4$ (295.7–414.0 ml)	5–7 (0.14–0.20 kg)
Adult	6–11 lb (2.7–5.0 kg)	Adult	1–1$^1/_2$ (236.6–354.9 ml)	3–5 (0.09–0.14 kg)
Senior	6–11 lb (2.7–5.0 kg)	Senior	$^1/_2$–1 (118.3–236.6 ml)	2–4 (0.06–0.11 kg)

* Refer to the Recommended Feeding Schedule on the manufacturer's package

Feeding the Adult Poodle

As your Poodle reaches adulthood at about one year, his nutritional requirements to maintain optimum body condition and weight will change. When he attains his full height, he will no longer need the high nutritional content of puppy food, and you can begin to feed him an adult maintenance diet. As with any diet change, this transition should be done gradually, by mixing larger portions of adult food with his puppy food until the puppy food is completely phased out.

As long as a commercial diet is not tainted with too many table scraps or treats and good feeding practices are observed, most dogs remain fit and healthy on an adult diet for many years. A dog in good condition appears well proportioned, with a slight layer of fat felt over the ribs. Dogs whose ribs, hip bones, or backbones can be seen or felt easily are underweight, and those whose body appears barrel-like with difficult-to-feel ribs are overweight. Either condition requires diet or feeding adjustments to bring the dog to a healthy weight.

Puppy Feeding Schedule

0–8 Weeks: Puppies younger than eight weeks old should have access to their mother's milk. This provides them with the nutrition and antibodies needed to fight illness and disease. At about three weeks old, puppies can be introduced to soft puppy foods, and at four weeks old they can be transitioned to dry puppy foods. However, they should not be completely weaned from their mothers until they are eight to ten weeks old.

8–12 Weeks: Puppies should be fed a quality puppy food three times per day. Remove food that is left uneaten after 20 to 30 minutes, and adjust feeding amounts according to your puppy's consumption.

3–12 Months and Older: Feedings can be reduced to two times per day. Monitor your puppy's weight, especially as he approaches one year of age, because he will be reaching his mature height, and the high-calorie puppy food may begin to cause him to put on excess weight. Toy and Miniature Poodles can be transitioned to adult dog foods when they are between eight and ten months old.

Toy and Miniature Poodles function well on twice-daily feedings.

Feeding the Senior Poodle

Although most dogs are considered "senior" after the age of seven, Toy and Miniature Poodles enjoy greater longevity than many other breeds, and they may not show signs of aging until nine or ten years of age.

Older Poodles may begin to experience some health conditions that require changes in diet. In addition, metabolism slows, and activity levels may decrease with age. For these reasons, it is important to monitor your dog's health and weight during his golden years.

Many dog food companies offer specially formulated dog foods for canine senior citizens. These foods are lower in protein, calories, and fat and can help prevent unwanted weight gain. They are also lower in sodium and phosphorous to help aging hearts and kidneys. Again, it is important to analyze the ingredients and guaranteed analysis on the label, because some senior pet diets use grain and soy products to achieve the lower protein levels in these foods.

Some dogs do just fine on an adult maintenance diet through most or all of their senior years, especially Toy and Miniature Poodles, who tend to expend as much energy as puppies as they get older. However, weight gain or other health conditions may indicate a diet change is needed. Some of the health conditions that may require a change in diet for the older dog include kidney, liver, digestive, heart, teeth, and skin problems. Your veterinarian can recommend the best diet to manage these conditions.

Sample Dry Food Feeding Schedule for Miniature Poodles*

Age	Weight	Type of Food	Cups Per Day	Ounces
6–11 Weeks	4–7 lb (1.8–3.2 kg)	Puppy	$1–1^1/_2$ (236.6—354.9ml)	4–6 (0.11–0.17 kg)
3–4 Months	6–10 lb (2.7–4.5 kg)	Puppy	$1^1/_4–1^3/_4$ (295.7–414.0 ml)	5–7 (0.14–0.20 kg)
5–7 Months	10–20 lb (4.5–9.1 kg)	Puppy	$1^1/_2–2$ (354.9–473.2 ml)	8–10 (0.23–0.28 kg)
8–12 Months	10–25 lb (4.5–11.3 kg)	Puppy	$1^1/_2–2^1/_2$ (354.9–591.5 ml)	6–10 (0.17–0.28 kg)
Adult	12–25 lb (5.4–11.3 kg)	Adult	$1^1/_4–1^3/_4$ (295.7–414.0 ml)	4–6 (0.11–0.17 kg)
Senior	12–25 lb (5.4–11.3 kg)	Senior	$^3/_4–1^1/_4$ (177.4–295.7 ml)	3–5 (0.09–0.14 kg)

* Refer to the Recommended Feeding Schedule on the manufacturer's package

FOOD-RELATED PROBLEMS

Proper management of your Poodle's diet can help avoid food-related problems, but problems still may occur, despite your best intentions. Toy and Miniature Poodles are particularly prone to develop problems with obesity and finicky eating, both of which often evolve unnoticed over a period of time.

Obesity

Obesity is the most common nutrition-related health condition in dogs, both in the United States and in Great Britain. Estimates say that 25 to 44 percent of companion dogs are obese, with the primary cause being an intake of too many calories. Dogs who are 15 percent over their optimum weight are likely to develop a number of health problems, including reduced liver function, high blood pressure, gastrointestinal disorders, heart disease, and joint problems. They are also at an increased risk to develop cancer and diabetes mellitus.

Obesity is an insidious condition that creeps up gradually over a period of time, with dog owners often unaware of the condition until it becomes blatantly obvious. Dogs who function fine on the same diet and measured portions of food for years may slowly begin to gain weight as their activity level and metabolism decline with age. It is important to have your veterinarian examine your dog annually, with weight changes clearly noted.

Sample Combination Dry/Canned Feeding Schedule for Adult Poodles*		
Weight of Dog	**Dry Portion**	**Canned Portion**
3–10 lbs (1.4–4.5 kg)	1.25 oz (0.04 kg)	1/10 can
10–20 lbs (4.5–9.1 kg)	2.8 oz (0.08 kg)	1/8 can
20–30 lbs (9.1–13.6 kg)	4.4 oz (0.12 kg)	1/5 can

*Refer to the Recommended Feeding Schedule on the manufacturer's package.

Prevention

You can get a head start in avoiding obesity by observing good feeding practices. Feeding on a regular schedule, measuring food portions, and providing regular exercise help keep your dog fit. Avoid feeding table scraps or leaving food in your dog's bowl during the day. If you have more than one pet, you *must* feed them separately, to monitor their intake. Easy ways to do this include using door gates to separate pets at feeding time, feeding pets in separate, enclosed rooms, or feeding each of them in their crates.

Treatment

The treatment for obesity should always begin with a thorough veterinary examination, since a number of underlying health conditions can cause weight gain, including hypothyroidism or diabetes mellitus. Blood tests can detect or rule out these causes so that you and your vet can develop an effective treatment plan.

Obesity due to excessive calorie consumption can be treated by reducing the quantity of food at mealtimes or changing your dog's diet to one that is higher in fiber and lower in fat. Moderate exercise is a necessary requirement for any successful weight-loss program. Just as obesity develops gradually, weight loss does not occur overnight. It takes patience and strict adherence to a treatment plan over the course of several months to a year before you see noticeable weight loss.

Other steps that can be taken in the battle of the bulge include reducing the consumption of treats or using low-calorie treats. For those who use treats as an effective training tool, you can replace this form of motivation with favorite toys and playtime. For some dogs, a favorite ball elicits just as much excitement as a chunk of chicken.

Finicky Eating

Smaller dogs, like Toy and Miniature Poodles, have a reputation of being finicky eaters. In reality, smaller dogs tend to chew their food more and do not gulp their meals like larger dogs. They have smaller mouths and smaller teeth. Because of this, smaller dogs prefer food that is easier to chew, such as moist or canned food. Dry food is now available in a smaller-sized kibble that is more appropriate for small-breed dogs. A little bit of warm water in your dog's kibble or a small amount of canned food added to his meal may encourage your dog to eat dry forms of food more vigorously.

If a dog is truly finicky—that is, if he stubbornly refuses to eat unless he is offered people food or other specific items with his meal, this could be due to patterns of behavior that have been established by the dog's owner. Dogs are not born finicky; they learn this behavior. And like most learned behaviors, it is easier to prevent the problem than it is to correct it later.

Exercising your Poodle regularly, as well as feeding him a healthy diet, will help prevent obesity.

Prevention

You can avoid creating a finicky eater by establishing

household rules forbidding the feeding of people food to your dog. Your dog's meals should not include table scraps, meat-based broths, or other enhancements. A dog will become accustomed to these practices, which can cause problems if you do not have these menu items available while traveling or when someone else must care for your dog. The biggest problem a finicky dog faces is that of nutrition. When other foods are added to a nutritionally balanced commercial dog food, the meal then becomes unbalanced and can lead to obesity or other health problems.

Treatment

If your dog has already become a finicky eater, your only recourse is to stick to a strict diet and refuse to cater to his whims. You may feel some distress when your dog refuses to eat for a period, but dogs do not starve themselves to death. Eventually, when your dog gets hungry enough, he will eat. It doesn't hurt to take certain measures to encourage eating, such as finding a brand of dog food that is more appealing to your dog or adding soft forms of dog food to make his meal more appetizing.

Begging

Feeding your dog people food is the greatest contributor to another common problem behavior: begging. Like finicky eating habits, begging is easier to prevent than it is to correct. This behavior seems to come so naturally to dogs that only one reinforcement for it is likely to create a well-established behavior. Indeed, it may have been the dog's inclination to beg that initiated and cemented his relationship with humankind thousands of years ago.

Prevention

In addition to forbidding the addition of table scraps and other people food to his meals, some strict table rules for family members can help you avoid this problem. Do not allow anyone to feed your dog from the table during meals. Also, avoid giving the dog any attention whatsoever while you are eating. Avoid petting, talking to, or even looking at your dog during meals. If he persists in staring at you or pesters you for attention, instruct the dog to lie down. Eventually, your dog will resign himself to the fact that your meal times do not include him, and he will lie quietly under the table until the meal is over.

You should also feed your dog before you sit down to eat. If he is satiated, less temptation exists to beg, and there is certainly no excuse for it. There is also less temptation for you to slip a few table scraps into your dog's meal after dinner if the dog has already been fed!

To prevent begging, refrain from feeding your dog from the table during meals.

Treatment

If your dog has already developed this undesirable habit, the best way to reschool him is to teach him the *place* command. Find a place away from your dinner table but within sight of it, and practice making your dog lie down there. Reward your dog with a healthy treat when he lies in his place. Eventually, make the dog stay in his place for longer periods, and reward him when he stays put. When the dog consistently responds to this command, you can begin to instruct him to go to his place during meals, but be sure to reward him immediately after the meal for his good behavior.

Your dog does not have a choice of what to eat or how much to eat, so the responsibility of providing a healthy diet, maintaining proper weight, and avoiding feeding problems ultimately falls on your shoulders. However, if you establish healthy feeding habits from the very beginning, your dog will enjoy the health benefits for the rest of his life. And you, in turn, can hopefully enjoy his company for many years to come!

Soft and Chewy Treat Recipe

2 $1/2$-oz (0.01 kg) jars of beef or chicken baby food (baby foods are low in sodium and sugar)

$1/4$ cup (59.1 ml) dry milk powder

$1/4$ cup (59.1 ml) wheat germ

Mix these items well, roll into balls, and place on a greased cookie sheet. Flatten them slightly with a fork, and bake at 350°F (177°C) for 15 minutes until brown. These treats can be refrigerated or frozen. Simple and easy to make, your dog is bound to howl for these chewy treats!

5

GROOMING
Your Toy or Miniature Poodle

One look at a meticulously groomed show Poodle is enough to intimidate the bravest of dog owners. Show dogs necessarily require a great deal of grooming care to prepare them for the show ring, and learning to create the exaggerated show clips does indeed take a lot of time, patience, and practice. Those who own Poodles for pets often resign themselves to the fact that professional grooming will be an ongoing expense in Poodle ownership. Fortunately, pet dogs can be groomed more practically than show dogs, and learning to groom your own Poodle is not as difficult as it may seem.

GROOMING AS A HEALTH CHECK

Whether or not you decide to use the services of a professional groomer, maintenance grooming between haircuts is still an important part of general Poodle care. Keeping a Poodle's hair in manageable condition makes grooming sessions more pleasurable for both dog and owner. At the same time, grooming also provides the opportunity to thoroughly examine your dog and evaluate his health.

Professional groomers are trained to be observant, and this can be a valuable skill for dog owners as well. Watch for any nose discharge, check the eyes for tearing or cloudiness, and don't be afraid to peek inside your dog's mouth to make sure his gums are healthy and pink. While going over your dog's body with a brush, make note of any lumps, skin tumors, swelling, or skin conditions that may require treatment.

GROOMING AS BONDING TIME

Any time you spend with your dog is bonding time. Whether you are playing with your dog, taking him for a walk, or even grooming him, you are strengthening your relationship with him. To get the most out of your grooming experience, use this time to nurture your relationship.

1. Train your dog how to behave appropriately for grooming by asking him to stand, sit, or lie down when needed. Training involves communication, and learning to communicate effectively with your dog will improve how he responds to you.
2. Kind words and gentle handling build trust and confidence. Speak cheerfully to your dog while grooming, and give him plenty of praise for his good behavior. Words of encouragement will help quell nervousness and apprehension.
3. Making grooming a pleasurable experience for your dog will teach him to enjoy the time and attention that grooming provides. Most dogs relish being brushed; it's like getting a back scratch or a body massage. Find your dog's pleasure areas, and give them plenty of attention. Brushing the back, rump, and neck will often get your dog squirming for more.

GROOMING EQUIPMENT

The most important aspect of Poodle grooming is acquiring the appropriate tools for the job. The proper grooming equipment can make the difference between a pleasurable grooming experience with a great outcome and a frustrating grooming experience that results in a horror of hair.

The most important aspect of Poodle grooming is acquiring the right tools.

Unfortunately, this means purchasing quality equipment, which can be a considerable expense initially. However, the right equipment can save you time and money in the long run.

Bathing tub with rubber mat

Brushes

Combs

Conditioner

Shampoo

Nail clippers

Tweezers or hemostat

Scissors

Electric clippers

Hair dryer

Grooming table

Imagine the difference between roofing a house with a hammer or a nail gun. Those who initially invest in a hammer are eventually convinced after days of blisters to buy a nail gun, spending more than they would have if they had bought the nail gun in the first place. The quality of the work you produce is in direct proportion to the quality of the tools you use.

If you are not sure you want to commit to grooming and clipping your own Poodle every six to eight weeks, or you're only interested in providing touch-ups between professional grooming sessions, by all means do not invest in a cache of expensive equipment. If you are serious about grooming your own show or pet dog, though, purchase the best equipment you can afford.

Bathing Tub

You will also need a place to bathe your dog, and thanks to the smaller size of Toy and Miniature Poodles, this does not have to consist of special facilities. Toy and Miniature Poodles can easily fit in the kitchen sink or a stationary tub. If your sink is not equipped with a spray nozzle, an inexpensive sprayer with hose can be purchased to attach to the faucet. A rubber mat in the sink will prevent your dog from slipping and becoming frightened.

Brushes

Two types of brushes are appropriate for Poodles. The most widely used is the *slicker brush*, which is rectangular in shape and has thin wire teeth set close together. This brush is invaluable for removing dead hair and mats and can even efficiently remove burdocks and other debris. It also separates the Poodle's fine, curly hairs to achieve a fluffy appearance. Another useful brush is the *pin brush*, which has thicker, longer wire teeth set in a flexible rubber base. This brush helps to penetrate longer hair, especially for the manes on traditional show clips or for maintenance brushing when the hair has grown longer between trimmings. Either brush comes in different sizes, so you must choose the one that fits your size Poodle. Medium generally works well for Miniatures, and small is more practical for Toys.

Combs

Combs also come in different styles and sizes. Combs with handles tend to prevent hand fatigue better than straight combs. At

A good comb is a necessity for keeping your Poodle's coat free of mats and tangles.

the minimum, you should have two combs: a general grooming comb with 1-inch (2.5-cm) metal tines spaced moderately apart, and a matting comb that has 1-inch tines (2.5-cm) spaced very closely together. The general grooming comb is a great all-purpose comb, but it also makes a great tool for removing hair from your slicker brush. Matting combs are useful for working out mats, pulling dead hair out of the coat, and removing debris.

Conditioner

Cream rinses and coat conditioners are necessary for professional grooming but optional for pet grooming. If your dog has extremely dry or coarse hair, these products can help moisturize and soften the coat. They do tend to increase drying time, but they can make the hair much easier to work with.

Shampoo

A huge variety of dog shampoos is available. Which product you choose depends on your dog's needs and your personal preferences. There are color-enhancing shampoos, fragrance-free and scented shampoos, medicated and flea shampoos, and odor-eliminating shampoos. But the kindest thing you can do for your dog, unless a specialty shampoo is needed for health reasons, is to choose a tearless shampoo that will not irritate your dog's eyes. Dogs are not particularly fond of baths, and irritating their eyes in the process is not going to make it any more enjoyable for them.

Nail Clippers

Nail clippers are available in two different styles, and which type you should get depends entirely on personal preference. Guillotine nail clippers have a hole in which to insert the dog's nail and a blade that slices across the hole. Scissors-style nail clippers

clip the nail off like a pair of scissors does. These tools, like many others, come in different sizes depending on the size of the dog, and small- and medium-sized nail clippers are appropriate for Toy and Miniature Poodles, respectively. Because nail clipping often leaves a rough edge on the nails that can be abrasive to human skin or can cause chipping or splitting of the nails, you may want to add a nail file or emery board to your grooming kit for smoothing out the nails after clipping. Some professionals use rotary tools to grind the rough edges of the nails, but while they are more efficient, they are also more expensive and require some skill to use. For pet owners, many nail clippers are sold in sets that include nail files, and these can accomplish the job adequately.

Tweezers or Hemostat

A pair tweezers or hemostat will help pluck hair from the Poodle's ear canal. (A hemostat is a scissors-like tool that can grasp hair firmly with its blunt-nosed, finely ridged grips.) Because the Poodle's hair grows continuously, removing hair from the ear canal is an important part of Poodle grooming. Excessive growth of hair in the ears can cause a number of health problems. To make this seemingly unpleasant job easier, you can purchase ear powder designed to make the hair stiff and brittle at the roots so that it is easier to grasp and remove.

Scissors

Quality quickly becomes evident in the clipping and trimming tools. Good-quality scissors cut the hair easily and neatly, while poor-quality scissors tend to push the hair through the blades, resulting in an uneven cut. Scissors come in different styles, and each provides certain advantages depending on what part of the body is being trimmed. A straight pair of barber shears is a good all-purpose scissors that can be used on multiple body parts. Blunt-nosed shears are great for working delicate or complex body areas, because they reduce the chance of poking the dog. Curved shears are handy for trimming the hair between the toes or sculpting rounded areas like pompons or the top of the head.

For beginners, a straight, blunt-nosed pair of shears should be the first investment. Other specialty shears can be added to your tool collection as you gain experience and confidence in trimming. Again, the size of the shears purchased should correspond to thesize of your dog. A 6- (15.2-cm) or 6.5- inch (17.8-cm) pair of shears works best on Toy Poodles, and a 7- (17.8-cm) to 7.5-inch (19.1-cm) pair of shears is more appropriate for Miniature Poodles.

Electric Clippers

The difference in quality of electric clippers is evident in their performance. A good- quality clipper penetrates the hair without dragging, has a quieter motor, and features a lower vibration level. The most popular manufacturers of professional-quality clippers

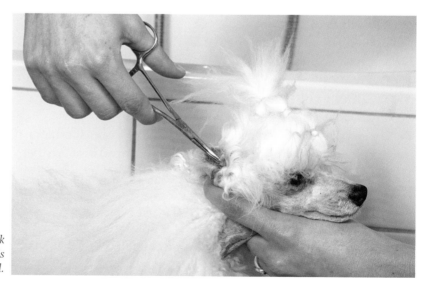

A hemostat will help pluck hair from your Poodle's ear canal.

also supply economy pet clippers for amateur use. High-end clippers have detachable metal blades, while low-end pet clippers have permanent metal blades that require the attachment of plastic combs to adjust the depth of the cut. A variety of clippers also fall within this range to accommodate any budget and satisfy any features preference.

Clipper blades for professional-quality clippers are sold separately, and a number of different sizes are necessary in Poodle clipping. At the minimum, the following size blades should be included in a beginner groomer's tool kit: #15, #10, #7, and #4. Show dogs will require the use of a #30 blade, but this blade should only be used by an experienced hand due to the extreme closeness of the clip. Professional groomers usually stock more than one of each size so that the blades can be rotated if they become overheated or dull. Pet owners, however, can get by with one of each size, since their equipment will not suffer the demands of professional grooming.

Metal clipper blades are limited in how long they can leave the hair, with the #4 being the longest cut at 3/8 inch (0.97 cm). Attachable plastic combs are available to provide cuts up to 1 inch (2.5 cm) in depth when they are attached to a #10 or #15 blade.

Hair Dryer

A hair dryer is a necessity for professional groomers and for pet owners who wish to create the fluffy hairstyle of a well-groomed Poodle. This can be one of the most expensive investments for the professional groomer, but pet owners can make use of

Clipper Blades		
Size	Hair Length	Use
#4	3/8 inch (0.97 cm)	Provides a moderately short body cut; good for general body clipping.
#5	1/4 inch (0.64 cm)	Provides a shorter body cut; good for summer body cuts.
#7	1/8 inch (0.33 cm)	Provides a very short body cut; good for summer cuts or for shaving hair from matted dogs.
#10	1/16 inch (0.15 cm)	This blade is good for close clips on the tail and sensitive underside areas. Also good for close cuts on the face and feet of dogs who are too sensitive to tolerate a #15 on these areas. It can also be used to shave patterns.
#15	3/64 inch (0.13 cm)	Usually used for close clipping of the face and feet. Also used in combination with plastic combs. This blade is preferred for show clips and can be used to clip patterns.
#30	1/50 inch (0.05 cm)	Extremely short clip used for show clips. Only professionals should use this blade.
#40	1/100 inch (0.03 cm)	Used for surgical clipping only.
#5/8	1/32 inch (0.08 cm)	This blade is 5/8 inch (1.6 cm) wide to create the narrow clipping path required in some specialty clips and patterns.

less expensive human hair dryers that have low-heat, low-air settings. Human hair dryers are not as convenient to use, because they must be held in the hand while trying to brush. They also tend to be noisy, which can upset some dogs. Professional dryers come in three different styles: cage dryers, floor models, and models that can be mounted to the wall or under the grooming table. Because Poodles must be brushed while drying, cage dryers are not used for professional Poodle grooming.

Grooming Table

A grooming table provides an efficient workspace for Poodle grooming. It is small enough to access the dog from any side, high

A grooming table provides a comfortable place for you to groom your Poodle.

enough to prevent back fatigue, and has a nonslip surface for the safety of your dog. Best of all, many of them can be folded up to save on storage space. In lieu of a grooming table, any elevated platform can be used, as long as it is sturdy and has a nonslip surface. Rubber matting can be purchased to convert any small, sturdy table or wooden box into a suitable grooming station.

Grooming arms are also available. These are inverted L-shaped posts that have an adjustable clamp on one end to attach to your grooming table. An eye-hook on the other end is used to attach a

restraining strap. This piece of equipment is not only necessary from a safety standpoint, because the strap can be placed around the Poodle's neck to prevent him from jumping off the grooming table, but it can also help keep the Poodle standing for grooming when the strap is placed around his waist (in front of the penis on male dogs).

Other Products

Other essential products for Poodle grooming include towels with which to dry your dog, ear powder to assist in removing hair from the ear canal, and a clipper spray, which lubricates and cools clipper blades. Styptic powder is a wonderful first-aid treatment for an accidental nick or to help stop the bleeding of a nail that has been trimmed too short. Even experienced groomers have small mishaps occasionally when a dog unexpectedly jumps or jerks while grooming.

HOW TO GROOM YOUR TOY OR MINI POODLE

Learning to groom your Poodle is a necessity, not an option, because a Poodle with a neglected coat can suffer tremendously. Regular brushing every week, nail trimming every month, and a full grooming treatment with bath and clipping every six to eight weeks should be on your calendar. Even though your Poodle's lovely curly hair does require a lot of maintenance, it does not have to be considered dreaded work. As you will discover, Poodle grooming can be an adventure.

Brushing

Weekly brushing with a slicker brush will keep your Poodle's coat fluffy and

Equipment Maintenance

Clippers and blades should be maintained according to the manufacturer's instructions. This usually consists of thoroughly cleaning the hair off the clippers after each use and oiling them occasionally to keep them operating smoothly. Blades should also be cleaned of hair after use and will need to be sharpened when they become dull. A dull blade will drag through and pull at the hair, causing discomfort for the dog and frustration for the groomer.

Blades, brushes, combs, and scissors should all be sanitized after use by dipping or soaking them in isopropyl alcohol or another disinfectant.

Brush your Poodle weekly with a slicker brush to keep his coat fluffy and free of tangles.

Grooming a Puppy

A visit to the grooming area of any dog show is an interesting experience. Dogs standing stoically still on grooming tables while groomers meticulously fuss over them is a common sight. However, dogs are not born with the patience and tolerance for such extensive grooming; they are trained to behave that way.

Poodle puppies should have their first clipping experience when they are between 8 and 12 weeks old, and they should be groomed regularly thereafter every 6 to 8 weeks. Putting off the first clipping after 12 weeks of age is likely to result in a very dirty, matted, and messy puppy, because the continuously growing hair will accumulate excessively by then. You should brush your puppy several times per week before his first formal grooming session to get him accustomed to having his various body parts handled.

Keep the first formal grooming session as short as possible so that the puppy can adjust to this new routine. A quick bath, drying, trim, and brushing are sufficient for his first experience. Handle the puppy in a businesslike manner so that he can learn that grooming time is not playtime. Words of encouragement and praise are in order when your puppy stands, sits, or tolerates grooming appropriately. Do not worry if the trim does not turn out according to your expectations, because you are not aiming for a Best in Show award. The goal of your puppy's first few grooming sessions should be to train him to behave appropriately and to keep his coat in manageable condition.

If the noise of the clippers frightens your puppy, you may have to desensitize him by letting the clippers run for a while until the puppy shows signs of relaxing. Then you can begin to set the clippers against his back until he becomes accustomed to the noise and vibration close to his body. Most dogs are not fond of the noise or air force of dryers, either, so it helps to dry the hindquarters and back first, saving the head and ears for last. Don't worry about getting your puppy completely dry during his first few grooming experiences. In the interest of keeping the first grooming sessions as short as possible, you can let your puppy partially air dry.

The feet and face tend to generate the most fuss with some dogs, so it is important to handle these areas frequently, even between clippings. A maintenance clipping of the feet and face between regular grooming sessions can help a puppy overcome his sensitivity in these areas.

tangle free. Although you can brush the coat in the direction the hair grows, this will flatten the coat. To achieve more fluff, make very short strokes in the direction of hair growth, and pull straight up at the end of your strokes. This will encourage the hair to stand up away from the body and give you the soft, touchable texture that makes Poodles so appealing.

Detangling Mats

The Poodle's curly hair is prone to mats if it is not brushed regularly. Mats can also develop very easily if the dog comes in contact with sticky substances, plant material, or dirt. It is best to avoid mats if possible, because matting damages the hair and can thin out the coat in the process of removing them. If you need to remove mats, though, a number of products are available to help loosen the hair and make mat removal easier, the most convenient of which is a spray-on tangle remover.

The tangle remover should be applied to dry hair and allowed to soak into the mat. Then you can attempt to separate the mat into smaller sections and brush the mat out of each section. If a mat is extremely large and tight, you may have to cut through it before you will be able to pull it apart. Starting close to the skin, use a straight shears to slice through the middle of the mat, and then separate the rest with your fingers. This, of course, will leave the hair uneven lengths, which you will have to correct with some creative trimming.

Bathing

Unlike other breeds of dog, Poodles require some preparation before bathing. They should be thoroughly brushed prior to a bath, because tangles and mats in their curly hair become tighter and more difficult to remove after they become wet. If your Poodle has accumulated a good length of hair, giving him a light trim before his bath will make it easier to penetrate his coat with shampoo and reduce drying time afterward. Many professional groomers put cotton balls in the Poodle's ears to keep water out of his ear canals. Keeping the ear canals dry makes it easier to remove the hair from them later.

Prior to bathing, you should have all your supplies organized. Shampoo, conditioner or other special treatments, towels, spray nozzle, and rubber mat should be assembled and ready to use. Be sure to test the water temperature, which should be comfortably warm.

When bathing your Poodle, you should work from the bottom up and from the back to the front. Begin by wetting your dog's feet and legs, working up toward the body. This is a

Use a tearless shampoo when lathering anywhere near your Poodle's eyes.

gentle way to acclimate your dog to the water temperature and wetness. Then wet the hindquarters and work up the back toward the neck. The head and ears should be kept dry until you are ready to wash them, because this will prevent the dog from shaking frequently during bathing. Shampoo the body and legs, working the shampoo into a thick lather and massaging it down to the skin with your fingertips. After you have rinsed the body thoroughly, you can begin to work on the head.

Only tearless shampoos should be used anywhere near the eyes. Just like the body, the shampoo should be worked in vigorously and rinsed thoroughly. Soap left in the coat will make the hair difficult to groom and clip and may dry out the skin. If you hold your dog's nose down while rinsing the head, water will not run into his nose and make him uncomfortable. Conditioner or special treatments can then be applied, followed by another thorough rinse.

Dogs seem to especially enjoy a vigorous towel drying. Let your dog have some fun with this, since grooming does not need to be a dour event. Squeeze the water gently from legs and feet, because water tends to accumulate on the lower extremities, and they take a long time to dry. A towel placed on your grooming table while drying your dog will help absorb some of the excess water from his feet.

Drying

Simultaneously blow drying and brushing the fur creates the soft, fluffy coat that is the Poodle's trademark. If the hair is allowed to dry too much before brushing, it will curl. As a result, you should begin with the body part that has the shortest length of hair, because this area will dry more rapidly than other areas. If your Poodle has a short body clip and longer hair on the legs, begin by drying the body first. The head and ears should be done last.

Direct the dryer's air to the part of the body you will be working on,

Drying the Face—Don't Blow Me Away!

Most dogs, including Poodles, do not like dryers blowing in their faces. When drying the ears, keep your dog comfortable by directing the dryer away from his face. When you are ready to dry the top of the head, start from the neck and work your way forward so that the air force of the dryer approaches the head from behind. Dryers that have variable speeds should be set on low velocity when working around the head. Have you ever noticed how difficult it is to breathe with a strong wind blowing in your face? A dryer blowing in your dog's face makes him just as uncomfortable.

and use your slicker brush to brush the hair back toward the neck, lifting straight up at the end of your strokes. This will train the hair to stand up rather than lay flat against the body. The slicker brush helps to separate and straighten the hair as it dries. Once the shorter-haired areas are dry and fluffy, you can begin to work on the longer-haired areas, including tail and leg pompons. If an area has dried and curled before you have had a chance to fluff it, you can use a spray bottle to mist the area again.

Show dogs are often trained to lie on their side for easy drying and brushing of the underbody. This is especially helpful in drying the traditional show clips that have long, heavy hair in the chest area. Pets sporting shorter body clips can have their undersides dried while standing. A grooming arm may come in handy to keep the dog standing while drying and brushing the underside and legs.

Clipping for Pets

Once your dog is completely dry, he is ready for clipping. This is the part of Poodle grooming that makes most beginners apprehensive. Keep in mind that every

When clipping the face, hold your dog's head steady with a hand around the side of the muzzle.

professional groomer was once a beginner, and when you take the first step, you are already on your way to becoming experienced. Just like Beethoven had to learn basic notes well before he could become an accomplished composer, you need to learn some basics about clipping and practice with simple clips before you can advance to more complicated grooming techniques.

Clipping the Muzzle

To clip the dog's muzzle, practice with a #10 blade and hold the muzzle under the jaw. Place the clipper across the bridge of the nose directly between the eyes. Then, clip forward in a smooth stroke to the end of the nose. Do not clip above the eyes, because the hair on the forehead is needed to form a rounded crown called a "top knot" when you are done. You can then hold the dog's muzzle from either side as you clip the rest of the muzzle from the eyes to the nose. When you get to the lips, stretch the skin slightly by pulling back the corner of the mouth before clipping. This prevents nicking the lips with the clipper.

Clipping the Face

When clipping the face, practice with a #10 blade and hold your dog's head steady with a hand around the side of his muzzle. The ear on the opposite side of his head can be drawn over the top of the head and held by the same hand to expose the side of your dog's face. Begin by placing the edge of the clipper level with the outside corner of the eye, and clip straight back to the ear. You can then clip the rest of the side of the face up to the ear line.

Clipping the Neck

While holding the top of your dog's muzzle, you can clip under the jaw to the neck. How far to clip down the neck is a personal choice. You can clip to the point where the head meets the neck or as far down as the breastbone, where the neck meets the chest. The important thing is to finish off the clipping line that runs from the ear to the underside of the neck in either a V-shape or a rounded line that is smooth and symmetrical on both sides.

The Basic Clip

A basic clip involves clipping short the face, feet, and base of the tail. These are the only areas of the body that require some clipping against the grain of the hair. Professionals prefer a #15 blade for clipping these areas, but beginners may want to practice with a #10 blade.

Clipping the Feet

The feet require a little more patience and practice to clip cleanly. Poodles do not always enjoy having their feet handled, which makes this job even more challenging. It is important to handle your Poodle's feet frequently. Do not be discouraged if your first few grooming sessions leave a few unsightly tufts of hair between the toes. It is better to learn this skill slowly and minimize the stress to your dog.

Place the clipper (#10 blade) at the base of the toenails, and clip up the toes to the ankle, dipping the clipper to the contours of the foot. Start at the center two toes and then clip each side toe. The back of the foot must be clipped a short distance from the main footpad to the ankle. It is very important to clip the hair between the pads on the underside of the feet. This hair tends to collect a lot of dirt and debris that causes it to mat. If left unclipped, hair between the pads can cause discomfort and lameness. Spread the pads apart by bending the dog's toes back slightly to make it easier to remove this hair.

To remove the hair between the toes, the toes must be spread apart. Then, use the corner of the clipper to clip each side of the toe. Take special care to avoid nicking the web of skin between the toes. If an abundance of hair makes it difficult to see the webbing, trim some of the hair with scissors first, and finish clipping with the clippers. If you are nervous about working a clipper on this part of the foot or your dog has not yet learned to be very tolerant of foot handling, be safe and use a blunt-nosed pair of scissors for this task.

Clipping the Tail

The tail is also clipped against the grain of the hair, starting at the middle of the tail and clipping to the base of the tail. For Miniatures, this should leave about 1.5 inches (3.8 cm) of the tail shaved. Toys will have about $3/4$ (1.9 cm) to 1 inch (2.5 cm) shaved. The underside of the tail and the area around the anus are very sensitive areas easily prone to clipper burn, so do not clip too close to the anus, and make sure your clipper blade is not hot or dull. Leave the hair long

The right clip can completely transform your Poodle.

on the end of the tail to shape a pompon. The only magic in getting a nice round pompon is in back-brushing the hair a little bit before trimming. Use your scissors to trim a little bit of hair off at a time, working in a circular motion as you sculpt the pompon.

Clipping the Body

The body is the easiest part of the dog to clip. Similar to shearing a sheep and twice as much fun, creating an even, all-over body trim takes little time and produces the greatest improvement to your dog's appearance.

The clipper blade should always be held flat against the body while clipping. If the blade is tipped down, it will leave an uneven cut and may poke the dog's skin. Always clip the body hair in the same direction as the growth of the hair. The blade sometimes causes the hair to flatten in this direction, but you can fluff it back up with your slicker brush and go over it with another pass of the clipper to obtain an even cut. A #4 blade will produce a body clip long enough to provide protection from sunburn and short enough to get some mileage out of your dog's haircut. If you prefer longer hair, a #15 blade can be used with attachable combs to produce any length hair you desire, but remember that longer hair must be trimmed more frequently to keep the coat manageable.

Beginning just behind the base of the skull, run your clippers down the length of your Poodle's back to the base of his tail. Clipper strokes should be long and smooth. The sides, shoulders, and chest can be clipped in the same manner. Do not clip down the thighs of the dog, because this is a part of the leg. The body should be clipped in a rounded arch over the thigh, so the leg hair can be left slightly longer than the body cut.

When you are ready to clip your dog's stomach, you can lift his front legs with one hand while clipping his underside with the other hand. Professionals usually use a #10 or #15 blade to clip the underside area between the back legs up to the last rib. This is another sensitive area in which the clipper must be run in the direction of hair growth, especially along the penis of male dogs. If you are apprehensive about using the clipper in sensitive areas, trim these areas lightly with scissors until you have gained more confidence. Blunt-nosed shears prevent your poking the dog, and using your hand to shield the genitals while trimming prevents nicking.

Trimming the Legs and Top of Head

With the body now showing a luxurious carpet of fleece, you can complete your grooming project by scissoring the top of the head and the legs. Creating a rounded top knot on the head is similar to trimming the pompon on the tail. Trim a little bit at a time, working your way around the head. Use the top of the ears, the eye line, and the base of the skull as the starting points in creating a round base, and then trim the top of the head to conform to this rounded shape. Fluffing the top knot with your brush occasionally will draw out any scraggly hairs to trim. You may or may not have to trim the ears, depending on how long the hair has grown or how uneven the ears are.

When trimming the legs, you can avoid unsightly cut marks by cutting the hair vertically. Use your scissors to blend the top of the legs into the body cut, and trim a straight hem around the ankle.

Hot Clipper Blades

Clipper blades heat up with use, so you should check your blade occasionally while grooming to make sure it is not getting too hot. A hot clipper blade can irritate your dog's skin or cause clipper burn, both of which will make your dog miserable and less inclined to tolerate grooming. If you think the clipper is getting too hot, let it cool down, spray it with a cooling product, or change to another blade.

Embellishments

As you and your dog become more comfortable with a grooming routine, you may want to advance your skills with a few embellishments to your pet clip. Here, you can personalize your dog according to your tastes by picking and choosing extra features that will make your dog subtly unique.

Moustache

A moustache can add a sense of sophistication to a Poodle clip. Usually reserved for male dogs, it also provides some gender identity. You can still shave a path down the top of the muzzle from the eyes to the nose, but when you clip the sides of the muzzle, shave only halfway to the nose. (Use a #10 blade.) Use your hand to pull the moustache forward so that you can clip the rest of the face symmetrically around it. Also, when you clip under the jaw, leave the hair on the chin.

You can trim the moustache in a number of ways to get the look you desire. The chin hair can be trimmed straight across, rounded into the moustache, or trimmed into a point for a goatee effect. Whatever you decide, you should trim the moustache to a reasonable length so that it is not so overbearing that it detracts from your Poodle's other features. Moustaches do tend to collect food and debris, so you will need to put a little extra effort into keeping it clean.

Belled or Tasseled Ears

This is a feature that can individualize your dog and also make the ears a little easier to maintain. By shaving the top portion of the ear, the bottom portion will flare out like a bell. Using the same blade you used to clip the face, clip from the base of the ear to about one-third down the ear. Clip the underside of the ear in the same manner. Afterward, trim the edges of the shaved portion of the ears with a straight pair of scissors to give them a finished look.

Leg Pompons

For a leg pompon to appear pronounced, the top part of the leg must be clipped short enough to give the pompon enough substance. Show clips involve shaving the hair on the upper part of the legs extremely close, but for a pet clip, the legs can be shorn to the same length as the body hair. Pompons look best on a pet clip that uses a shorter body cut, like that accomplished with a #5 or #7 blade. Another requirement is that the hair on the lower portion of the leg has had a chance to grow to a sufficient length to produce a pompon.

When clipping the body, clip the legs down to the knee and hock joints. The pompons will encircle the legs from the knee to the ankle and the hock to the ankle. Before trimming the pompons, fluff them out with a brush. Then, scissor around the widest part of the pompons to make them cylindrical. You can then trim the top and bottom of the pompons to give them a rounded appearance. Because gravity has a way of making the hair droop somewhat, trim only a small amount around the top edge of the pompons while trimming a much more rounded edge on the bottom. This prevents your pompons from looking misshapen when they sag a bit.

Specialty Shampoos

You can use specialty shampoos to enhance your Poodle's natural color.

Coloring

Coloring a Poodle does not necessarily mean grooming a Poodle into the likeness of a punk rock star. Sometimes it is just a matter of enhancing a Poodle's natural color with the use of specialty shampoos. Products are available to deepen the shade or eliminate gray from any of the established Poodle colors. If not available at your local pet supply store, these products can be found at any outlet supplying professional grooming products and equipment.

For those who feel compelled to make a more noticeable statement, white and cream Poodles can be colored using natural vegetable dyes or chalk, with the results limited only by the groomer's imagination. This can be a fun experiment for dog owners and an interesting way to dress up your dog for special occasions or parades.

Vegetable dyes (food coloring) should be mixed with water to achieve a darker shade than actually desired, because the color will be diluted when applied to the dog. The color is then applied with a sponge and distributed evenly with a brush. Chalk can be applied directly or can be soaked prior to application and then drawn onto the dog and allowed to dry. These are temporary colors that wash out easily, so you must keep in mind that your creation will run and fade if your dog becomes wet. Semi-permanent colors are not recommended and should only be applied by professional groomers if they

With her practical, hands-on experience, a grooming mentor can teach you how to groom a show Poodle.

are used at all, because some dogs may be sensitive to the chemicals or fumes.

Clipping for Show

Grooming a Poodle for show is a skill acquired only through proper instruction and practice. Many tricks of the trade include learning which products to use for color enhancement and coat conditioning and learning trimming and banding techniques to disguise slight imperfections in conformation. This kind of information can only be obtained from experienced exhibitors, professional instructors, or literary references devoted to the subject.

Finding a mentor is a wonderful way to learn how to groom a show Poodle. Mentors can provide practical, hands-on experience as you assist with grooming preparations. Many exhibitors are passionate about promoting and educating others about their breed, and they are willing to help others get started in the sport of showing. Your dog's breeder may be able to refer you to someone who is interested in mentoring, or you can check with your veterinarian or local Poodle club.

Anal Gland Care

All dogs have anal glands just below the base of the rectum. These glands accumulate a highly malodorous waste product that is normally expelled when the dog defecates. However, it is not uncommon for Poodles to fail to eliminate this product, causing an impaction of the anal glands. This condition can be very painful, because the anal glands become hard and infected. Therefore, it is a good idea to check your dog's anal glands regularly and remove the anal gland contents when necessary.

You will know that your Poodle has impacted anal glands if you feel a hard mass in the anal glands or if your dog displays discomfort, excessive licking of the anal area, or drags his rump along the floor. Because you can damage the anal glands if you empty them improperly, you must first consult with your veterinarian on how to empty them safely. After you have learned the procedure, you can empty them

yourself. This is not a particularly pleasant job, because the scent of the anal gland contents is very offensive. Most professional groomers prefer to empty the anal glands while bathing so that the foul-smelling substance can be washed away immediately. To empty the anal glands yourself, squeeze just below the anal opening with your forefinger and thumb, and push in a slight upward motion to draw out the contents.

Ear Care

Poodles accumulate hair growth in the ear canals that must be removed. Ear powder helps to stiffen the hair and make it brittle so that you can easily pluck it out. You can remove hair with your fingers by grasping a little bit of hair at a time and pulling it out. This is generally not a painful procedure for the dog, although he may be a little sensitive to it the first few times. You can also use tweezers or a hemostat to remove hair from the ear canal, especially when the hair is too deep to reach with your fingers, but take care not to poke the dog. Again, remove a small amount of hair at a time with these tools.

Once the hair is removed, a cotton ball dipped in alcohol

Light-colored Poodles are prone to tearstains, but you can remove them using cornstarch or a variety of commercial products.

can be used to remove any remaining wax or dirt. Swelling, redness, discharge, or odors are signs of an ear infection that require a consultation with your veterinarian for treatment.

Eye Care

Light-colored Poodles tend to develop brown tearstains under their eyes. You can remove most of this stain by shaving the hair off the face, and the rest can be removed using a variety of commercial products developed for this purpose. You can also use cornstarch to safely disguise the stain.

Blow drying, brushing, and clipping sends tiny fibers of hair into the air that can get in your dog's eyes and irritate them. Using a commercially available eyewash after grooming helps prevent eye irritations and infections. Some products are designed to wash out the eyes as well as remove tearstains, so you can attend to both eye care needs at the same time.

Nail Trimming

Nail trimming is a very important part of Poodle maintenance care, because overgrown nails can cause the toes to lift or splay and can result in lameness. Whenever a problem with the feet is present, it can affect the dog's legs, joints, and posture. Extremely neglected nails can grow so long that they curl under the foot and become embedded in the pads of the feet, a seriously painful condition for the dog. However, even mildly neglected nails can create problems. The quick, which is the fleshy, nerve-rich center of the nail, tends to lengthen when nails are allowed to become overgrown, making it difficult to trim the nails as short as they should be cut.

The quick is easiest to locate on dogs with white nails. It will appear as a dark shadow inside the nail, and the nail can be carefully clipped to avoid cutting into it. For dogs with dark nails, a little bit of the nail can be clipped at a time until a small dark spot appears in the middle of the clipped surface. Another way to determine how much to clip on a dark-nailed dog is to gauge the excess growth by looking at the underside of the nail. Because the top of the nail grows faster than the bottom, the nail develops a hook underneath. The base of this hook gives a good indication of how much nail you can safely trim.

While many dogs dislike having their nails clipped, Poodles who experience regular nail clipping and foot handling from a young age are more likely to accept this part of grooming without any problems. Nail clipping sometimes makes inexperienced dog owners nervous, because clipping the nail too short can cause profuse bleeding and pain for the dog. Fortunately, there are safe and easy ways to clip your dog's nails.

Always clip your dog's nails in a well-lighted area, and do it when your dog is in a calm mood, such as after a nap. He will be less likely to fidget and cause injury to himself during nail clipping if he is not excited or full of energy. Place each nail into the hole of the guillotine clipper or position your scissors-type clipper across the nail, locate the quick, and cut off the tip of the nail. (If you accidentally nick the quick, apply styptic powder to the nail to stop the bleeding.) It is better to leave the nails a little too long than to cut them too short. You can always remove a little more nail with a nail file or clip the nails more frequently if you can't get them short enough.

Signs of Dental Disease

Bad breath (halitosis)

Red or swollen gums

Loose teeth

Discolored teeth

Mouth pain

Refusal to eat

Loss of weight

Yellow-brown buildup of tartar and plaque

Receding gum line

Pus or other discharge from the gums

Gums that bleed easily

After clipping the nails, file the rough edges to prevent chipping or splitting. In line with the Poodle's unofficial status as a fashion statement, the nails are sometimes painted with a quick-drying nail polish to achieve certain effects. This might be a matter of establishing contrast, such as painting a white Poodle's nails black. It can also involve color coordinating, such as painting a black Poodle's nails red. Very little is taboo when it comes to personalizing a Poodle, as long as you don't cause the dog harm or discomfort.

Dental Care

Dental care has become one of the most important maintenance responsibilities for dog owners. With 80 percent of dogs showing some sign of gum disease by the age of three, veterinary organizations have embarked on educational campaigns to draw attention to the importance of regular dental care. Dental care is particularly important for Toy and Miniature Poodles, because this breed has a reputation of accumulating tooth plaque and developing dental problems.

Dogs are not prone to cavities as humans are, but they do tend to accumulate tartar and plaque at the gum line that can lead to periodontal disease. Bacteria thrive in the calculus formed by tartar and plaque and can cause receding gum lines, loose teeth, and infections. Severe infections can even enter the bloodstream and affect internal organs.

Chewing on bones and tartar-control products helps keep the teeth clean, but this does not reach the part of the tooth at the gum line. The only practical way to remove plaque at gum level is to brush your dog's teeth. Incorporating oral care into your grooming routine is an easy way to ensure that it is done regularly.

Toothpaste manufactured specifically for dogs is a necessity, because human toothpastes are not palatable for dogs and can make them sick if swallowed. Dog toothpastes are usually flavored with beef or chicken, and letting your dog taste a little bit prior to brushing may convince him that dental hygiene isn't such a bad idea. Many dog toothpastes are supplied in a dental kit that includes a toothbrush or a finger applicator. If you use a human toothbrush, it should have the softest bristles available and should be a child's size for Toy and Miniature Poodles. Most dogs do not have a problem with tooth brushing, especially if they become accustomed to it at a young age. A dog's teeth should be brushed at least once a week, but several times per week is better.

When you are ready to begin a tooth brushing routine, let your dog lick some of the toothpaste off your finger, then attempt to brush the front teeth only. Hold up his lips with one hand while brushing with the other hand. For subsequent tooth brushing sessions, you can gradually add more teeth to this routine until your dog eventually tolerates having all his teeth brushed. It helps to hold up the lips to access some of the teeth, but most dogs do not enjoy having their lips stretched far enough for you to get at the molars. For these teeth, it is best to get the toothbrush inside the cheek for brushing. Concentrate on removing food residue from the outer surfaces of the teeth, because the dog's tongue can clean the inside surfaces sufficiently.

In addition to your home dental care regimen, your veterinarian should examine your dog's teeth annually. She will be able to determine if professional cleanings are warranted. Performed under general anesthesia, a professional cleaning removes plaque from below the gum line and polishes the teeth to make it more difficult for plaque and tartar to adhere to the tooth surface. For dogs who are particularly prone to plaque and tartar buildup, several special diets are available to assist with oral health. Your veterinarian can recommend a special diet if it is necessary.

A sense of pleasure is to be gained in keeping your dog happy, healthy, and beautiful. A well-groomed dog can be a considerable source of pride for his owner. More than that, grooming promotes a stronger bond between dog and owner through interactions during the grooming process, as well as interactions afterward. A clean dog is known to be received more closely by humans, particularly those who love him. So, if you love your dog, groom him!

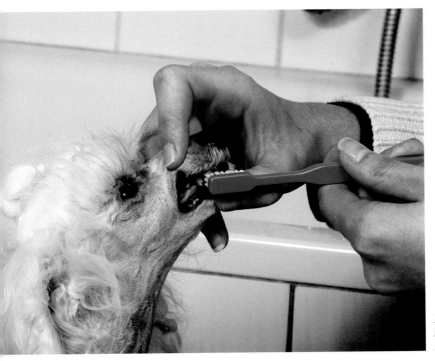

Promote good dental hygiene by brushing your Poodle's teeth at least once a week.

TRAINING AND BEHAVIOR
of Your Toy or Miniature Poodle

raining is one of the biggest responsibilities of dog ownership, but the time and effort you put into it determines the greatness of the rewards you reap. Teaching your dog how to behave helps him live harmoniously in your household, prevents accidents, and keeps neighbors and guests happy. Best of all, training helps build a strong human–canine relationship by developing trust, respect, and confidence.

PRINCIPLES OF TRAINING

Four main components are used to shape behavior: rewards, consequences, repetition, and consistency. A training program that lacks any one of these components is not a comprehensive training program and will suffer in its effectiveness. Certain training practices also can enhance communication, produce better results, and make training an enjoyable activity for both dogs and their owners.

Rewards

Rewards, of course, exist to encourage appropriate behavior, and they can consist of treats, favorite toys, petting, praise, or playtime. For rewards to be effective, you must offer them immediately, so that the dog can associate the reward with his behavior. In the interest of letting the dog know instantaneously when he has displayed the correct behavior, many trainers now use clickers to let the dog know he will be rewarded. This can also be accomplished by saying the word "yes" when a dog behaves correctly, followed by offering the promised reward. Praise should always be delivered in your happiest, most upbeat tone of voice. If treats are used, you should choose a treat that is sufficiently appealing to motivate your dog, but not so alluring that your dog cannot concentrate on the task at hand.

Consequences

Consequences help discourage inappropriate behavior. Consequences have received a bad rap due to their negative nature and the horror of past training methods that employed unnecessarily harsh methods. However, even positive training methods must use consequences if they are to be effective. Modern training methods use gentler forms of consequences, such as withholding rewards or attention. And like rewards, consequences must be imposed immediately in order for the dog to associate them with his behavior. This is why punishing a dog *after the fact* is not effective.

If a behavior has already occurred, as in the case of a dog who gets into trouble when his owner isn't present, it is best to ignore the behavior and take steps to prevent it from happening in the future. Also, never impose consequences if the dog behaves inappropriately while learning a new skill. This only serves to dampen his willingness to learn. Only use consequences when a dog consciously disobeys a learned skill.

Repetition

Repetition is required in any learning process. Not only does it facilitate the retention of what is learned, but it also provides

practice to improve performance. Learning theorists call this *classical conditioning*, and indeed, repetition conditions our dogs to behave the way we desire. Puppies require more repetition than adult dogs, because their juvenile minds do not have the retention abilities of a mature dog. Even after a skill is learned, occasional repetition keeps a dog's skills in top form.

Praise your Poodle effusively when he does something well.

Consistency

Consistency prevents confusion. For example, if

you feed your dog scraps from the dinner table one night and admonish him for begging the following night, the mixed messages you are giving sabotage your attempts to train your dog not to beg. When training is executed in a consistent manner, the dog learns what is expected of him, and he also knows what to expect of you. Consistent communication is a source of security for a dog, because most dogs only want to please their humans.

BEFORE YOU TRAIN

Toy and Miniature Poodles are exceptionally perceptive and communicative, and the person who makes the effort to understand her dog will find greater success in training.

In fact, adhering to some basic training principles will prevent breakdowns in communication and help you to achieve your training goals together.

Training Tips

The following basic training principles will help you and your Poodle achieve your training goals:

1. Learn patience
2. Teach hand signals
3. Establish eye contact and name recognition
4. Keep training sessions short

Learn Patience

Patience is not necessarily a requirement of training, but it can certainly make teaching and learning more pleasurable for you and your dog. If you find yourself losing patience, it is best to stop the training session and try again another time. You should always try to end a training session on a positive note. Ask your dog to perform a simple exercise that he already knows well, reward the dog, and then end the session.

Teach Hand Signals

Hand signals are often used in formal training, in addition to voice commands. Teaching your dog to respond to hand signals can come in handy when working with him from a distance or when noise levels are high. They are also required for advanced obedience training. Hand signals often evolve from the exaggerated hand movements used to manipulate a treat in the process of training, but they become more subtle as a dog learns the skill.

Dogs tend to learn hand signals quite readily. Because they are not capable of a complex spoken language, as humans are, they rely quite heavily on visual cues and are experts at interpreting body language. For this reason, dogs often respond better to hand signals than voice commands, but it is important for your dog to learn to respond to both. If you use hand signals, then you should give the voice command and hand signal separately, not at the same time (preferably, the voice command first). Hands are a wonderful human feature, but they are often quite busy. Thus, when you cannot use your hands to instruct your dog, voice commands are essential.

Basic Obedience Hand Signals

No standard hand signals are used in dog training. Many hand signals evolve naturally during the training process, such as placing a hand on the floor as if placing a treat there to encourage a *down*. You can develop any kind of hand signal that most closely follows your training technique and is easiest for your dog to associate with a skill.

The following hand signals are the most common signals used in basic obedience training:

- **Come:** Wave your hand toward your body in a "come follow me" motion.
- **Sit:** With your flat palm facing up, raise your arm from the elbow as if lifting a dumbbell, drawing your palm to your chest.
- **Down:** With your palm facing down, make a level, downward motion with your hand.
- **Stay:** With arm outstretched, your flat palm should be facing your dog as if you were stopping traffic.

Establish Eye Contact and Name Recognition

As a method of communication, training is not effective if you do not have your dog's attention. If you try to talk to someone who is on the phone, reading a book, or watching television, she may only hear a fraction of what you say.

Likewise, if your dog is distracted, you cannot communicate with him effectively. It is important to establish eye contact with your dog before asking him to perform a skill.

A good way to establish eye contact and teach your dog to respond to his new name at the same time is to reward him every time he looks at you when you say his name. Throughout the day, say your dog's name frequently, and reward him each time he looks at you. This conditions him to be very responsive to his name. Then, when it is time for training, you can say your dog's name to get his attention.

Keep training sessions short and frequent to prevent your Poodle from becoming bored.

Keep Training Sessions Short

Training sessions are most productive when they are short and frequent. If you try to feed your dog too much training at once, he may become frustrated or bored. At this point, his mind will begin to wander, and any further training will be ineffective. With this in mind, limit training sessions for puppies to ten minutes. Adult dogs can usually tolerate 15 to 20 minutes of training at a time. You can keep your dog focused during training by varying the skills you are working on so that your dog does not become bored with performing the same task repeatedly.

To get the most value out of your training, sessions should be conducted a minimum of three times per week to provide enough repetition. It also helps to limit the number of new skills you are teaching, because trying to teach too much too fast can result in confusion. Perfect the skills you are working on before moving to something new.

TRAINING THE PUPPY

Your puppy is like an empty canvas. He knows very little about life, and it is up to you as his surrogate parent to paint the world for him. A considerable amount of work is involved in teaching a puppy what he needs to know about living with humans, but there is also a lot of satisfaction in creating the masterpiece that is to become the dog of your dreams.

Socialization

Socialization consists of life experiences that shape a dog's perception of the world. It contributes to the development of social skills that can affect how a dog responds to people, other animals, different environments, different situations, and even training. Proper socialization also helps a dog develop confidence, stress-coping mechanisms, and independence, all of which can profoundly affect his behavior.

A dog who is not adequately socialized may become fearful or aggressive. He may become easily stressed and have difficulty coping with changes in his life. These behavioral issues are not easily solved, because social skills must be learned at an early age while the brain is still able to form new connections. If a dog does not receive adequate social experiences during his first year of life, he may not be able to acquire important social skills later.

Toy and Miniature Poodles who are handled frequently before they are weaned will have a greater affinity with humans than those who are not. If human handling is postponed until they are 8 to 12 weeks old, they can still develop close human attachments, but it may take longer. After 12 weeks of age, it becomes increasingly more difficult for a dog to relate to humans. Other social skills, such as how to tolerate or react to other dogs, strange people, and new environments can be learned by providing plenty of social opportunities throughout your puppy's first year.

How to Socialize

Expose your young Poodle to as many people, animals, and

Socialize your Poodle by exposing him to as many different people and situations as possible.

places as possible. Take your dog for walks, and be sure to stop and say hi to neighbors. Participate in charity dog walks where other dogs will be in abundance, or take your dog with you to a pet store that allows dogs on the premises. Visit accommodating friends and relatives who won't mind if you bring your dog with you. Take advantage of any opportunity that allows your dog to experience a variety of sights, sounds, and smells. He literally needs to get out to see the world. Dogs who are isolated and confined to a small territory, such as the home, are at a high risk of developing social deficiencies.

Crate Training

Crate training helps your puppy feel comfortable and secure in his crate. This can provide a number of benefits for the dog owner, who may then be able to use the crate to assist with housetraining or for confinement when traveling or showing. Formerly den animals, dogs can learn to tolerate and even enjoy spending time in a crate, especially if they are acclimated to a crate at a young age.

Perhaps the biggest misuse of crates is to use them to confine a dog for long periods while the owners are at work. Only use the crate for short-term confinement, no more than a few hours at a time. Keeping a dog confined to such a small space for long periods is not good for a dog's physical and emotional health. For longer periods of confinement, it is best to use a puppy pen or small room.

How Long Should You Crate Your Puppy? General Guidelines

Age	Maximum Length of Time for Crating
8–12 weeks	Up to 1 hour
12–16 weeks	Up to 3 hours
16–24 weeks	Up to 5 hours
24 weeks and up	Up to 6 hours

When choosing a crate, it is important to get the right size for your dog. The crate should be just large enough for your dog to stand and turn around comfortably. Dogs generally do not like to soil the place where they sleep, but getting a crate that is too large may result in the dog using a portion of it to potty. If you have a puppy, however, you may want to get a crate large enough to accommodate him as an adult. For Toy Poodles, this would be approximately 12 inches (30.5 cm) by 19 inches (48.3 cm) by 10 inches (25.4 cm), or size small by most manufacturers' standards. Miniature Poodles should use a crate that is approximately 14 inches (35.6 cm) by 23 inches (58.4 cm) by 12 inches (30.5 cm), or size medium.

How to Crate Train

To begin crate training, place the crate in a prominent location in your home, and leave the door open so that your puppy can explore it if he wants. The crate should have some form of soft bedding inside, such as a blanket or fleece liner. If your puppy is not showing any fear of the crate, start putting treats just outside the crate door and eventually inside the door to encourage your puppy to put his head inside. Gradually place the treats farther inside the crate to convince the puppy to enter it. Do not try to push your puppy too fast during this process, or you may make him fearful.

When your puppy is comfortable entering the crate to retrieve a treat, practice putting some of his favorite toys inside the crate for him to retrieve. Throughout the crate training process, you should encourage your puppy to explore, play, and sleep in his crate so that he can learn that it is his personal territory. When he seems confident about entering and exiting the crate on his own, attempt to feed him in it by placing his food dish just inside the entrance. Again, gradually move the food farther into the crate until your puppy is eating his meals inside. When you have reached this stage, you can begin to close the crate door while your puppy is eating and then open it immediately when he is done.

The next stage of crate training involves conditioning your puppy to spend longer periods in the crate. Always make sure your puppy has had a potty break prior to crating him, and then put him in his crate for 10 or 15 minutes while you are at home. These crating sessions can become successively longer if your puppy is tolerating them well. Treating and praising your puppy when he enters the crate willingly encourages him to cooperate. If you give your dog the *kennel* command, and give him a treat while he is entering the crate willingly, he will soon learn to enter his crate on command.

When choosing a crate, make sure that you get the right size for your Poodle.

The next step is to crate your puppy for short periods of time when you leave the house. Tell your puppy to kennel, and reward him when he does. You should not fuss over your puppy prior to leaving or upon your return. Keep departures and arrivals as subdued as possible. Putting a chew toy or treat-releasing toy in the crate will help keep your puppy busy and comfortable while you are gone. You should continue to crate your puppy occasionally when you are home, so that he does not associate crate confinement with you leaving him alone.

Do not crate your puppy for more than two to four hours at a time, depending on his age and stage of bladder control. You do not want your puppy to get in the habit of eliminating in his crate. When not in use, leave the crate open for your puppy to use at will. He will begin to accept the crate as his safe refuge and not something to be dreaded.

Housetraining

Housetraining can be a frustrating experience for the dog owner whose expectations are too high. It does take some time to housetrain puppies, because they do not have the bladder control of adult dogs. Do not expect your puppy to be completely housetrained until he is at least six months old. Some mistakes will occur, which should be expected, and how you handle these lapses will affect the efficacy of your training. The fact that many puppies are left alone for long periods during the day while their owners are at work can complicate training, but this situation, too, can be managed in a way that will not detract from your training efforts.

How to Housetrain

You can take certain steps to make training go more smoothly and quickly. The most essential is to keep your puppy on a regular schedule. Plan to feed and exercise your puppy at the same times every day. Schedule outside potty breaks immediately after eating, sleeping, and exercising, because these are times when your puppy will most likely need to eliminate. You should also have a specific

Take your Poodle to the same area for potty breaks, because the scents there will encourage him to eliminate.

If your puppy must spend a good portion of the day confined, paper training may be the best option for you in the beginning. To paper train your puppy, place newspaper over the area in which you would like him to eliminate. If your puppy makes a horrible mess of shredded paper during the day, please remember that this situation is temporary. He will initially eliminate wherever the urge hits him, but he will eventually begin to use a preferred area. You can then begin to shrink the papered area until it is a more manageable size. Always save a section of paper with urine to lay down with the clean supply, because the scent provides the stimulation necessary to encourage your puppy to continue using the paper. If your puppy is confined to a room with an outside door, you can gradually move the papers closer to the door so that he will go to this area when he needs to eliminate. This makes it easier to transition him to going outside, so that you can eventually remove the papers.

area to take your dog for potty breaks, because the scents there will encourage him to eliminate. Every time your puppy eliminates in the designated area, praise him lavishly.

If you issue a command such as "go potty" or "do your duty" each time your dog uses the appropriate area, he will begin to associate the command with the act of elimination. An elimination command is a good way to let your dog know where he is allowed to go, and this also lets your dog know if your outside excursion is intended for business instead of play. Always remember to reward your dog afterward for the correct behavior.

In addition to his regularly scheduled potty breaks, take your puppy outside at least every hour initially and supervise him closely in between. Do not allow your puppy to have unrestricted access to your house until he is reliably housetrained. The most noticeable signs that your puppy needs to relieve himself are stopping what he is doing to sniff around or pacing back and forth with his nose to the ground. Whenever you are unable to supervise your dog to watch for these signs, he should be kept in a confined area.

You should *never* punish your puppy for housetraining lapses. This only serves to make him fear you. Ignore accidents, and clean them up without a fuss. If you are fortunate enough to catch your puppy in the act, immediately scoop him up and take him outside to his potty area. Even if he no longer has to go, this helps him associate the act with the proper place.

FORMAL OBEDIENCE CLASSES

Although novice dog owners in their own homes can easily teach basic obedience skills, the value of formal obedience classes cannot be overstated. The obedience class environment provides distractions and experiences that cannot be duplicated at home. Dogs who are trained in the home learn to be obedient in the home environment, but they may not respond as reliably in other situations. Obedience classes can improve reliability by providing training experiences in a different location, around other dogs, and amid a variety of other distractions.

For the dog owner, formal obedience classes offer personal instruction and guidance from a professional trainer that can help solve specific training problems. For the dog, there is no better place to become socialized than the controlled environment of a

training class. Because training is conducted in a foreign environment, it tends to increase the level of trust and respect between a dog and his owner.

Choosing a Trainer

Finding a good dog trainer can be an overwhelming task. Each trainer uses slightly different training methods and possesses strengths and weaknesses in her field. Sometimes it is a matter of finding someone who shares the same philosophies of training and has personality traits that complement your own. However, you should consider a few other things when evaluating the trainers in your area.

- **Dog training instructors should use only positive training methods.** Any program that still employs inhumane training methods is outdated and indicates that the trainer has a lack of current education. Jerking the leash, hitting, choking, helicoptering (swinging a puppy around by the leash), or alpha rolling (forcing the puppy onto his back) are primitive methods of training. Positive training, on the other hand, relies on positive reinforcement to encourage appropriate behavior and subtle but effective consequences to discourage inappropriate behavior.
- **A good trainer is one who is just as good at training people as training dogs.** Good communication skills and an in-depth knowledge of dogs are the most important qualities of any good dog trainer. Designation as a Certified Pet Dog Trainer (CPDT) from the Association of Pet Dog Trainers (APDT) or memberships to other dog training associations don't necessarily guarantee quality, but they are a good indication that the trainer takes her job seriously.
- **Sometimes the only way to determine if a trainer meets the criteria of a good trainer is to sit in on some training sessions to observe.** Reputable trainers encourage prospective students to scrutinize their classes. This gives you the opportunity to note how many students are enrolled and how much individual attention they receive. You should also observe the general mood of the class, which should be a fun and educational experience for the dogs and their owners. Impatience, anger, frustration, and stress can ruin a dog's will to learn and turn training into a dreaded chore for dog owners.
- **The best trainers adapt their training program to the dog,**

Creating the Perfect Pet

Training can make the difference between owning a dog who is a cherished pet and owning one who is a terror on four legs. According to a survey conducted by the National Council on Pet Population Study and Policy (NCPPSP), over 90 percent of the dogs relinquished to animal shelters never received any formal obedience training.

rather than expecting the dog to adapt to the training program. This means that each dog is treated as an individual, and training methods are adjusted accordingly. Trainers who use a one-size-fits-all approach to training are obviously not going to be as successful as those who tailor their programs to meet the needs of the individual dogs and their owners.

Choosing a Training Program

Training programs come in different formats, such as group classes, private sessions, or in-home sessions. Group classes are the most common, the least expensive, and the most beneficial for those who desire formal instruction in basic obedience. They allow students to observe other dogs and their owners, and they provide training in a distracting environment that can improve a dog's reliability and consistency. Private sessions are useful for those who have particular training goals and need individual instruction, while in-home sessions are usually reserved for those who have specific training issues most often associated with household behaviors that require professional assistance.

Training formats that do not include the dog owner are not recommended. It may seem convenient to hire someone to train your dog for you, but you will not gain the knowledge and experience that comes from training your own dog. Because obedience requires ongoing practice to keep skills intact, you must learn the training techniques necessary to continue reinforcing the learned behaviors. But more important than that is the fact that a dog responds best to the person who trains him. Training develops a relationship and level of communication that cannot be attained in any other way. Do you want your dog to be obedient and reliable for his trainer, or do you want your dog to have this kind

Choose a trainer who uses positive training methods.

of relationship with *you*? This is why it is a good idea to include the whole family in your dog's education; your dog will learn to respect and respond to other household members, and all members of the household will learn the methods and skills covered in the classes. Such consistency contributes greatly to a well-trained dog.

Enrolling in a Training Class

Once you have chosen a trainer and decided on a class format that best suits your needs, you will have to enroll in a class appropriate for your dog's age. Puppy classes are designed for puppies under six months of age. They employ training techniques that are more effective for very young dogs, and they also cover specific behavior issues associated with puppyhood. Adult dog training classes are appropriate for any dog over six months of age.

Most basic obedience classes for either puppies or adult dogs require a commitment of six to eight training sessions held once per week. Each session generally runs between 45 minutes to an hour. The cost of formal obedience training varies, and you can expect to pay considerably more for private or in-home lessons.

BASIC OBEDIENCE TRAINING

Basic obedience is considered the foundation on which all forms of advanced training are based. For pet owners, basic obedience training teaches the bare essentials for good manners. Whether you decide to enroll in training classes or train your dog at home, the following basic commands help you establish some control over your dog's behavior. This control is a valuable asset in solving any specific problem behaviors you may encounter in the course of dog ownership.

Come (Recall)

The *come* command is the most important obedience command you can teach your dog, which is why obedience classes often stress the *come* command and practice it frequently. A dog who does not come when called is a danger to himself and others. He risks getting lost or hit by a car, not to mention the fact that he will become a neighborhood nuisance and possibly subject his owner to fines.

Basic Commands

The following basic commands will help you establish some control over your dog's behavior:

- Come (recall)
- Sit
- Down
- Stay
- Walk on a loose leash

Reliability in your dog's response to the *come* is the goal of recall training, and it does take some time and a lot of conditioning to achieve. Because this command is used to control the dog in many different situations, it must be practiced in many different locations with a variety of distractions.

Teaching Come

Initially, work with your dog in the home by calling him occasionally and rewarding him when he comes. Call your dog from different rooms and at different times of the day, always indicating that he has responded correctly with a "yes" and rewarding him. He will quickly learn that coming when called is in his best interest.

When working outside, practice the recall with your dog on a long line. Let your dog wander to the lengths of the line and then call him to you and reward him accordingly. Because the goal is to encourage your dog to *want* to obey you, always call him in a cheery voice, and encourage him with claps or other noises. When off leash in an enclosed area, encourage your dog to come to you by running away from him while calling his name. This may arouse his desire to chase, and he will come back in your direction.

If you can find an assistant to help you, practice the recall by having the assistant hold the dog on a leash. Find a position some distance away, and then call the dog using verbal encouragement and running away from the dog. The assistant can release the dog as he responds to the recall, but only practice this in a safe, enclosed area in case the dog becomes distracted.

You must *never* punish a dog for coming when called, even if he was initially disobedient. This is one of the biggest mistakes made in recall training. Do not call your dog to you prior to

The sit command is a prerequisite to learning other obedience skills.

administering any form of punishment, because this destroys your dog's desire to come when called. When your dog comes to you under any circumstance, praise him generously.

Sit

The *sit* command is surprisingly useful for getting an excitable dog under control. It is also a prerequisite to learning a number of other obedience skills. There are several ways to teach this command, and you should use the method that feels most comfortable to you and works best for your dog.

Teaching Sit

The first method involves holding a treat above your dog's head and moving the treat just behind his eye level while instructing him to sit. As he lifts his nose to keep his eyes on the treat, his back end will naturally drop, and he may end up sitting automatically as a matter of comfort. If he does, let him know he has responded correctly with a "yes," and reward him.

It should only take a few rewards to ignite the lightbulb in your dog's head, because sitting is a very natural position for dogs, and most learn this skill quite readily.

Down

A dog who learns how to lie down on command has a great start in household manners. You'll be able to instruct your dog to lie down when people are seated at the table for dinner, when he is getting a little too excited around guests, or when it is time to go to bed.

Teaching Down

The *down* command can easily be taught from the *sit* position. When your dog is sitting, hold a treat on the floor in front of him. As he lowers his head to get the treat, move the treat away from him so that he will have to stretch out to get it. Very often, a dog will stretch out his front legs until he is in a lying position.

Some dogs learn particular skills in stages. If your dog lowers

Teach down *without physically forcing the position.*

his body even a little bit while teaching the *down,* or moves his front feet forward without actually laying all the way down, you should still give him a "yes" indicator of correct behavior and reward him. With practice, he may eventually drop his body into a complete *down* in an effort to achieve comfort. If not, gently pull his front feet forward to help your dog understand what you expect. Putting pressure on his back or shoulders is likely to be met with resistance, so it is best to teach this skill without physically forcing the position.

Stay

The *stay* command is an exercise that *must* be learned in stages. Progressing too fast will require you to start over from the beginning. Take your time and back up a few steps in your training each time your dog does not stay as told. This skill has two components that you must teach: distance and time. A dog needs to learn to stay regardless of your distance from him, and he also needs to learn to stay for a period of time until released from the command. Like the *come* command, the *stay* is also a skill that you should teach in a variety of locations to ensure reliability. Training in your home can be conducted off leash, but a leash or long line should be used outdoors.

Teaching Stay

Begin with your dog sitting in front of you, and then instruct him to stay, using a hand signal if desired. Move one or two steps backward from your dog, and then immediately step forward to reward him if he doesn't move. The length of time you require your dog to stay should be brief in the beginning, because teaching *stay* is a gradual conditioning process. If your dog does well, you can begin to increase the distance a couple steps at a time while also increasing the length of time you expect your dog to hold the *stay.* After each successful *stay,* return to your dog to reward him for his compliance.

Walk on a Loose Leash

Dog walking is one of the most common and enjoyable activities for dog owners. It is a great way to get some exercise and fresh air and to socialize with neighbors. At the same time, nothing is more annoying than a dog who constantly pulls on the leash. Returning home with a sore arm and stiff shoulder is enough to take most of the fun out of a pleasurable stroll, and even though Toy and Miniature Poodles are not heavyweight brutes of the dog world, some of them can still give a pretty strong, steady tug on a leash, making dog walking an uncomfortable experience.

Dogs have a faster pace than humans. When allowed to explore off leash, they will bound ahead as if in a great hurry to get somewhere. As a result, when they pull on a leash, they are simply attempting to move at a speed more natural to them. An effective consequence for this behavior is to deny them the pursuit of the direction they are going until they realize they will not get there any faster by pulling. Appropriate rewards for keeping pace with their humans are also in order.

Establishing Household Rules

Establishing household rules ahead of time will help your dog understand what is expected of him.

Teaching Walk on a Loose Leash

To encourage your dog to stay close to you, hold a treat by your side as you walk and reward your dog frequently when he walks on a loose leash at your side. Each time your dog pulls on the leash, abruptly turn around and start walking in the opposite direction. This interrupts the behavior and get the dog's attention. It also makes it clear to the dog that he will not be getting anywhere by pulling. Reward your dog when he again approaches your side.

If you have a higher goal than simply teaching your dog to walk on a loose leash, use this same method to teach your dog to heel. This is a more precise obedience skill in which the dog handler holds the leash in her right hand while the dog walks close to the handler's left side. Encourage your dog to stay close to your left side by holding a treat in your left hand, and reward your dog frequently for maintaining his position there. If your dog gets out of position, turn around and walk in the opposite direction while commanding him to heel. When he comes back up to your side, reward him.

HOUSEHOLD MANNERS

The moment your dog comes home, he will begin to learn how to live in your household, whether you intend to teach him or not. Therefore, it is important to establish household rules ahead of time and solicit training participation from all members of the family. It is much easier to teach your dog limits in the beginning than it is to change his behavior later.

Off the Furniture

Toy and Miniature Poodles are lapdogs, a term that means they often sit on or near their people. Considered a shedless breed, most people do not mind allowing them on the furniture. However, don't forget that dogs coming in from a wet outing don't realize they should keep their muddy paws off the couch. Consistency dictates that if you allow your dog on the couch, you must *always* allow him on the couch. Thus, you may have to clean your dog up when he comes in from outside or put a protective covering on your furniture to prevent problems with your dog's furniture privileges.

Allowing your dog on the couch does not mean that you have to allow him on *all* of the furniture. Lying on the couch is not the same as jumping up on the coffee table. You may not like the idea of a dog imposing his own space on your bed at night. In these cases, teach your dog which pieces of furniture are off limits.

Solution

When your dog goes onto forbidden furniture, command him to *off*, entice him to vacate the furniture with a treat, and

reward him when he complies. Rewards do not always have to consist of treats, but treats may work best when it comes to teaching your dog to stay off the bed. In this scenario, it helps to convince the dog to use his own bed by telling him to *off* the furniture and directing him to his bed with a food reward. He will soon understand where he is supposed to sleep.

Treats are a great motivation for keeping your Poodle off the furniture.

Rushing out the Door

Some dogs get into the habit of rushing out open doors. This can be an extremely dangerous habit if the dog has not yet learned his yard boundaries, and he risks the chance of getting lost or hit by a car. Dogs have been known to get tails and feet slammed in doors, which can cause significant injuries, and they can knock down little children or trip adults who are using the door. This can also be an extremely annoying behavior when company comes to call.

Solution

To stop or prevent this behavior, you must work with your dog on a leash. Open the door a bit while blocking the opening with a leg. Instruct your dog to stay. If he shows any inclination to bolt through the door, stop his exit with your leg, close the door, and start over. If he waits, reward him. Progressively enlarge the door opening, and keep rewarding your dog for waiting. When you are ready to let him go through the door, release him from waiting with an "okay."

Poodles learn this skill rather rapidly, and you should practice it with every door in the house. It helps to reinforce this training any time your dog goes through a door, including visits to the veterinarian or groomer.

Areas Off Limits

There may be some areas in the home that you do not want your dog to access. This might include places where garbage is kept or where another pet's food is located.

Solution

This situation can be addressed by teaching your dog the *out* command. When your dog enters a forbidden area, instruct him to *out*, and usher him quickly out of the area. As soon as he is within his acceptable boundary, praise and reward him. Walk into the forbidden area to see if your dog follows. If he does, usher him back out again and praise him when he is outside his limit. When your dog begins to understand that the area is off limits, further test him by walking into the area while carrying a dog toy. If he does not enter the area to follow you, he deserves a plentiful reward.

Confining Your Dog

Until your Poodle is fully boundary trained, keep him fenced or leashed for his safety.

One thing to keep in mind about indoor boundary limits is that your dog cannot be expected to respect these limits when you are not home. Dogs do not have the same self-control as humans and will react to temptations if left to their own devices. The soft couch in the living room, the cat's food on the porch, or the garbage in the utility room will be more than most dogs can resist. So keep doors closed or put up door gates to keep your dog out of these areas when you leave the house.

Outdoor Boundaries

Teaching a dog his yard boundaries is a matter of convincing your dog to restrict his territory. Because young dogs love to explore, and adult dogs take some time to accept a new home territory, training a dog to reliably respect his yard boundaries takes time and sometimes maturity to achieve. Until a dog is fully boundary trained, you must be vigilant in keeping your dog fenced or leashed for his own safety. Thankfully, Poodles are not known to be wanderers, and they much prefer to stay by their people. Castrating and spaying further reduces the desire to roam and makes boundary training much easier.

Solution

The foundation for successful boundary training is teaching the *come* command. A dog who is trained to come reliably can be called back if he ventures beyond his boundaries. With consistency, he will eventually internalize his boundary limits. But the integral ingredient for success is reliability in responding to the *come* command, and this takes a lot of conditioning to achieve. You should not attempt outdoor boundary training off leash until your dog has reached this level in his obedience training.

In the meantime, do some preliminary work to help instill boundary limits. While walking your dog on a loose leash, walk around the perimeter of your property. If your dog wanders across the boundary, give him the *out* command, and pull him back gently if he does not respond. Just as with indoor boundary training, he will begin to learn where he is not allowed to go. A convenient time to do this is before or after going for a walk. You can use the same method as you did for indoor boundary training to teach your dog which outdoor areas are off limits, such as gardens and other sensitive or dangerous areas of your property.

PROBLEM BEHAVIORS

When it comes to dealing with problem behaviors, keep in mind that dogs do not engage in inappropriate behaviors to get even with us, even though they may be trying to tell us something. Understanding canine behavior can help solve these problems by use of prevention, diversion, and conditioning.

Most problem behaviors are more easily solved if your dog is first educated in basic obedience. Besides establishing a level of behavioral control, basic obedience commands are often used to substitute appropriate behaviors for inappropriate ones. This is another example of how basic obedience instruction serves as a good foundation for any other type of training.

The following are some problem behaviors that your Toy or Miniature Poodle may experience, as well as some suggestions for solving them.

Play Biting

Puppies naturally roughhouse with their littermates and mother, biting them, nipping at them, and tugging on them. While this kind of play is perfectly acceptable when they are playing with other dogs, it is not a desirable way to play with humans. A puppy's sharp teeth can damage human skin, and as the puppy grows larger, this damage can become more severe. A dog who has not learned to keep his mouth off people has a higher tendency to develop aggressive or defensive biting later on.

Say Yes Instead of No

When a new puppy or dog joins a household, there is much he needs to learn. Until he has learned household rules and proper manners, his owner may be challenged with a variety of troublesome behaviors. It is very easy to fall into the habit of screaming, "No!" when he gets into trouble, but this word can become overused and misused, resulting in a lack of effectiveness.

Positive guidance can help you change the focus from telling your dog what not to do, to telling your dog what to do. Replacing the word "no" with consistent commands produces much better results. For example:

- When your dog jumps on forbidden furniture, direct him to get off.
- When your dog takes food off the coffee table, issue the *leave it* or *don't touch* command.
- If your dog enters a forbidden area, command him to *out*.
- When your dog has a desire to chase something or cross boundaries, remind him to stay, or call him to come.
- If your dog enjoys stealing your personal property, tell him to *drop it*, *leave it*, or *come* so that you can retrieve the item.
- During housetraining, tell your dog *outside* if you catch him having an accident, and take him outside immediately, even if he has already finished eliminating.

Solution

To teach your dog that play biting is not an acceptable way to play, discourage your puppy from using his mouth on you. Tell him, "No bite" when he engages in this behavior, and withhold your attention for a moment. Your puppy must learn that you will not play with him if he bites you. For puppies, playing is the whole purpose of life. Making the fun end is the strongest consequence you can apply. In addition, it gives the puppy a time-out to settle down. You can also encourage your puppy to play bite one of his toys instead of your hands by shaking the toy in front of him to encourage him to take it in his mouth.

Children should be highly supervised when playing with a puppy, because they often get a puppy overexcited, which can lead to excessively rough play that leads to biting. Children who are too young to understand how to get a puppy to stop play biting may end up inadvertently encouraging the puppy to play this way. Parents may need to step in to provide some guidance for appropriate play, or they should separate the kids from the puppy for a cooling-down period if necessary.

Chewing

Chewing is most common in puppies, because they enjoy exploring the tastes and textures of objects in their environment. They also need to chew to relieve the discomforts of teething. They do not understand that some things are dangerous to chew and that other things will cost their owners a good sum of money to repair or replace.

Solution

Supervising your puppy and restricting his access to your house will help you control chewing damage. The need to chew

diminishes as a dog matures, but even adult dogs have an instinct to gnaw on hard or abrasive surfaces to help them clean their teeth and massage their gums.

You can prevent inappropriate chewing by providing a variety of appropriate chew toys. Offer your

You can prevent inappropriate chewing by providing your Poodle with suitable chew toys.

puppy or dog a selection of toys that feature different shapes, textures, and hardness levels. This way, he will have plenty of choices to suit his chewing needs. Products designed specifically for chewing, and textured dental chews, such as Nylabones, provide the most benefits for oral health.

Consumable chew products like rawhide and pig's ears are very appealing to dogs, but while rawhide has been a favorite among dog owners due to its long-lasting quality, it is also one of the most difficult consumable products for dogs to digest. If your dog experiences frequent digestive upset, rawhide may not be suitable for him. Pig's ears, although easier to digest, do not last quite as long and may have to be cut into smaller pieces to accommodate the size of Toy and Miniature Poodles. The consumption of any edible chew product should be limited so that it does not cause problems with your dog's diet.

Prevention also consists of removing objects from the environment that are tempting chewing targets. You may have to keep your shoes in the closet, because some Poodles have a keen fascination for shoelaces. Also, do not use human items as toys for your dog. Dogs do not discriminate between old socks and new ones, so it is not a good idea to teach a dog that socks are acceptable playthings.

If you catch your dog chewing on something inappropriate, do not punish him. Instead, redirect him to an appropriate chew item. If he begins to target things that cannot be removed from the environment, such as furniture or rugs, you can use a number of deterrents. Repellent or boundary sprays can be applied to furniture at risk. Tabasco sauce can also be an effective deterrent, but only if it will not stain the item it is supposed to protect.

Why Do Puppies Chew?

Puppies chew because they enjoy exploring the tastes and textures of objects in their environment. They also need to relieve the discomforts of teething.

Digging

Dogs dig for a number of reasons. They may dig to satisfy an instinctual urge to pursue prey, to relieve boredom or stress, to escape confinement, or sometimes just to create a cool place to lie down. Fortunately, Poodles are not usually heavy diggers, although they may develop the habit as a form of entertainment.

Solution

Prevention consists of not leaving your dog outside for long periods of time without supervision. You can reserve a couple of toys for outside use so that your dog will have more appropriate activities to do. If your dog receives plenty of exercise and attention, he is less likely to discover digging as a form of amusement.

If your dog has already gotten in the habit of digging, supervise him closely so that you can stop the behavior when it arises and redirect him to an appropriate activity. Punishment is not recommended, because it will exacerbate the problem for dogs who dig to relieve stress. Some dog owners have found relief by constructing an appropriate place for their dogs to dig. A sandbox located in a shady or sheltered area can provide an acceptable place for digging. Burying treats in the sand will encourage your dog to use the sandbox, and it will provide a convenient option for redirection.

Submissive Urination

Submissive urination may occur when a Poodle greets someone in typical enthusiastic fashion and dribbles urine as if he is too excited to control his bladder. This is actually a common greeting behavior for dogs who want to make it clear to new acquaintances, both canine and human, that they do not pose a threat. It is a submissive cue accompanied by other submissive gestures, such as laid back ears and a crouched body.

This is a common behavior for puppies, perhaps because they understand their lower rank in the social order, and the puppy

Supervise your dog while he is outdoors to keep him from digging.

usually outgrows the behavior as he matures. But a few individuals persist in displaying this behavior into adulthood. More common with females than males, and especially prominent in dogs with a submissive nature, submissive urination can be an annoying, messy problem.

Solution

The most effective way to handle this behavior is to instruct visitors to ignore the dog until he has had a chance to calm down. Avoiding eye contact with the dog is especially important, because this is all it usually takes to trigger this behavior. In extreme cases, you may need to confine him when guests arrive. This gives your dog some time to adjust to the presence of newcomers before allowing him to greet them.

Coprophagia (Stool Eating)

Coprophagia is another behavior exhibited in puppies that is often outgrown. A dog may develop the unsavory habit of eating feces, either that of his own or that of another species. The cause of this behavior continues to elude experts, although a number of theories exist. Some believe it may be caused by a nutritional deficiency, while others think it may be a learned behavior. But the fact remains that no one really knows why some dogs develop coprophagia and others don't.

Besides providing a source of disgust for dog owners, coprophagia can cause a number of physical problems for dogs. Consuming feces contributes to diarrhea, which can upset the best housetraining schedule, and it can also cause stomach upset and flatulence. Even worse, the dog may acquire parasites or illness, especially when feces of wild animals are consumed. Without the advantage of knowing a specific cause, it is impossible to devise a foolproof treatment plan, but dog owners can do a few things to minimize the problem.

Solution

The first course of action should be prevention. Keeping the dog's outdoor areas clean by picking up any excrement immediately removes the source of temptation from the environment. Supervising the dog while outdoors allows you to prevent the consumption of waste material. If the dog tends to eat his own feces, diet supplements are available to make his own feces unpalatable to him.

This problem tends to diminish with maturity, somewhere between one and two years of age. However, don't be surprised if the habit reappears occasionally. Coprophagia tends to resurface during cold seasons for reasons unknown to veterinarians and behaviorists, but it will likely decline again during the warmer months.

Jumping Up

Jumping up on people can be a common problem with Toy and Miniature Poodles. Because they love to greet people, it is often difficult for them to control their exuberance at your homecoming or the arrival of guests. Dogs naturally greet their canine playmates in this fashion, but people are not dogs and do not have the same kind of appreciation for this type of greeting. Luckily, Toy and Miniature Poodles are too small to knock down children or injure the elderly. Nevertheless, it is still an annoying habit and one that can do significant damage to pantyhose.

Solution

You can solve this problem by making your dog sit for greetings. You can keep a bowl of treats near the front door and

enlist your guests to assist you when they arrive. If your dog sits nicely when people come to visit, give him a treat or reward him with petting. If he jumps up, the recipient of this behavior should turn away from him, avoid eye contact with him, and withhold all attention. Eventually, your dog will learn to sit nice for petting when people arrive.

If your dog has exceptional difficulty controlling his urge to jump, you may have to put him on a leash prior to opening the door for guests. You can then prevent his jumping while

Jumping up can be a common problem with Toy and Miniature Poodles.

practicing the *sit* exercise. For some Toy and Miniature Poodles, any form of physical contact is more than they can emotionally handle, and it will cause them to lose control, in which case you may have to avoid petting as a reward, and your guests will have to ignore the dog completely until he settles down. Puppies are too immature to have much self-control, and it may take considerable time to teach them not to jump up. Nevertheless, it is important to discourage this behavior consistently from the beginning so that it does not become well established. Patience, persistence, and consistency will reward you with a well-mannered pet.

Did You Know?

Jumping up can be a common problem with Toy and Miniature Poodles because they love to greet people.

Barking

Barking is another behavior that you should address early on, before it becomes well established and difficult to stop. Poodles like to bark. Like a hair trigger, it doesn't take much to set them off. On the one hand, this quality makes them excellent watchdogs, but on the other hand, excessive barking can be annoying for anyone within earshot, including your neighbors.

Although you can control barking to some extent, it cannot be completely eliminated. If your goal is to have a quiet dog, you've picked the wrong breed. Most people have a limit to the amount of barking they can tolerate, and controlling barking is a matter of letting your dog know what that limit is. Conversely, dogs also have a minimum amount of barking they feel is necessary to give proper warning. Allowing your dog to give ample warning before expecting him to stop is the key to successful control.

Solution

When your dog has voiced enough warning, you can issue the *quiet* command, distract him from the stimulus that caused him to bark, and reward him if he ceases barking. You can only expect your dog to cease barking if the stimulus that caused him to bark is regressing in intensity. For instance, if a strange person were approaching your door, it would be unnatural and probably impossible for a Poodle to stop barking while the person advances closer. It is much more reasonable to expect your dog to stop barking if the person is walking away. Keeping these principles in mind will help you understand your dog's barking behavior and allow you to make reasonable requests of him.

Dogs bark as a method of communication, and a Poodle owner

should always be alert to what her dog may be trying to tell her. Barking is not always a reaction to a stimulus. Sometimes a dog just wants to get your attention. Dogs who bark as a reaction to loneliness or frustration may be suffering from separation anxiety, in which case other remedies are required to solve the problem.

Separation Anxiety

Separation anxiety occurs when a dog has difficulty coping with being left alone. Although this type of problem can develop with any breed of dog, Toy and Miniature Poodles are exceptionally attached to their owners and do not always cope well with being left alone for long periods. A number of problem behaviors have been associated with separation anxiety, including destructive behaviors, urinating, defecating, or barking. The cause is often associated with the dog's need for companionship in relation to his history as a pack animal. Dog owners who spend a good portion of the day at work can find themselves in a challenging situation when attempting to meet the companionship needs of their dogs.

Solution

Fortunately, the dog's history also helps provide some solutions. As former hunters, dogs are most active at dawn and dusk, and they are naturally more lethargic during the day. Providing adequate exercise in the morning and evening is one of the best preventive measures available. If your dog can expect and receive regular exercise at these times, he is less likely to develop problems.

Keeping your dog comfortable during the day is the best way to reduce stress. In addition to being well fed, exercised, and given a potty break before you leave, your dog should have a comfortable bed, appropriate toys, and fresh

Keeping your Poodle comfortable during the day is the best way to reduce stress.

water available while you are gone. A regular feeding and potty break schedule helps to regulate his system and avoid housetraining lapses.

Your dog should not have unrestricted access to your house while you are gone unless he can be completely trusted. Restrict his space to a particular room, and gradually add more space after he is housetrained and has bypassed the teething stage. When your dog appears ready to have the run of the house, check your home for any sources of temptation before you leave. Make garbage containers inaccessible, put away shoes and other chewable items, don't leave food on tables or counters, and close bathroom doors if your dog has a fetish for toilet paper.

Most animal behaviorists believe that the key to treating separation anxiety is to reduce the dog's anxiety level by making the owner's comings and goings less traumatic. This consists of keeping departures and returns extremely subdued. Avoid long, emotional good-byes, and do not fuss over your dog upon your return. Give your dog a chance to settle down before giving him any attention.

In extreme cases, an owner can perform frequent "mock departures" to further desensitize the dog. This consists of putting on a coat, jingling keys, and opening and shutting the door without actually leaving. This helps to reduce the dog's anxiety, because he will not be able to associate departure routines with being left alone.

Dogs are not born with the instincts or knowledge that tells them how to cohabit with humans. We must teach them the skills they need to be good pets. Learning how to communicate effectively with your Poodle allows you to teach him everything he needs to know. Then, all it takes is time and patience to mold your dog into the perfect pet you've always wanted.

Seeking Professional Help

Most dog owners experience some behavior issues that must be dealt with at some time or another. While a majority of problems can be solved with proper socialization, training, and sometimes a little creativity on the part of the dog owner, those occasions arise when conventional remedies are not effective. Some problems may be beyond the expertise of your obedience instructor or veterinarian, in which case you may need to consult a specialist.

The first place you should inquire about referrals for animal behaviorists is at your veterinarian's office. It is imperative that health conditions be ruled out as a cause of behavior problems, and this can only be done through a veterinary consultation or examination. Many veterinarians also specialize in animal behavior, so the vet's office could be your one-stop solution for canine problem behaviors.

Despite a lack of regulatory control, animal behavior specialists can offer invaluable support for dog owners experiencing difficult canine problem behaviors. The growing base of knowledge in this field is making it easier for dog owners to keep their pets rather than surrender them to animal shelters. Just as a physical illness cannot be treated without first arriving at a correct diagnosis, solving problem behaviors begins with understanding the underlying cause.

ADVANCED TRAINING AND ACTIVITIES

With Your Toy or Miniature Poodle

f you truly enjoy spending quality time with your dog, advanced training and other activities are the perfect way for you to have fun with your dog while gaining a greater mutual understanding and developing a deeper bond.

AKC CANINE GOOD CITIZEN® TEST

The AKC Canine Good Citizen (CGC) program was developed by the AKC as a way to address the needs of all dogs and their owners. The test promotes responsible dog ownership and helps dogs become respected members of their communities. Both purebreds and mixed-breed dogs are welcome to participate.

CGC certification is awarded to dogs who pass a ten-step test designed to evaluate a dog's skills in basic obedience and general manners. It also demonstrates the handler's responsible attitude toward dog ownership. The CGC has become a standard part of the evaluation process for dogs certified through therapy dog organizations and has also been used in conjunction with other training programs. Dogs who are certified are often welcome in establishments that otherwise do not allow dogs, including hotels, nursing homes, and hospitals. The benefits for dogs, their owners, and the community in general are obvious, which explains the program's far-reaching and steadily growing popularity.

A dog who passes the CGC test must possess self-control, competency in basic obedience, and social skills. Many training facilities now offer specific classes devoted to training CGC skills, although they often require basic obedience training as a prerequisite.

The CGC test is administered at various training facilities by approved AKC evaluators. Check with local trainers or the AKC to find a registered evaluator in your area.

THERAPY WORK

Toy and Miniature Poodles have a high aptitude for therapy work because they enjoy the company of people and are very perceptive. They can easily learn skills required for this work, their clean coats are especially suited for the health care environment, and their small size is nonthreatening and offers patients the opportunity to hold and cuddle them. Nevertheless, there are some things to consider.

Toy and Miniature Poodles require proper handling to avoid injury, and contact with children or the elderly must be closely supervised to avoid overly rough handling. Poodles with a high energy level may have difficulty controlling their excitement in meeting new people, and if they jump on people, they can injure the fragile skin of the elderly or infirm. Sometimes training and maturity are all it takes for a dog to show his true therapy potential, but some dogs within every breed do not make good candidates for therapy work.

AKC Canine Good Citizen® Test

Test 1: Accepting a friendly stranger

Test 2: Sitting politely for petting

Test 3: Appearance and grooming

Test 4: Out for a walk

Test 5: Walking through a crowd

Test 6: Sit and down on command/staying in place

Test 7: Coming when called

Test 8: Reaction to another dog

Test 9: Reaction to distractions

Test 10: Supervised separation

To receive the CGC certificate, dogs must pass all 10 items of the test.

Source: The AKC Canine Good Citizen Test Evaluation Form

Characteristics of a Good Therapy Dog

A good therapy dog prospect is well socialized and enjoys human attention. He should not be shy, fearful, or aggressive. If a dog has the necessary personality traits for therapy work, he will still require training to teach him the proper manners and prepare him for the various situations he will encounter. He must be able to sit nicely for petting or brushing, and he should be schooled in basic obedience. He should be able to get along with other dogs, and he will have to learn to tolerate wheelchairs and other medical equipment.

Characteristics of a Good Therapy Dog Owner

Dog owners, likewise, must fulfill certain requirements. They must learn how to conduct themselves in the course of dealing with facility staff and residents. They should also be willing to devote time to this activity on a regular basis, because nursing home residents and hospital patients look forward to consistent visits. For dog owners willing to make the commitment, therapy work is a great opportunity to share your special canine companion with others and contribute to the common good of your community. It is a great way to meet people, keep active, and spend time with your dog, all at the same time.

Types of Therapy Work

Most people envision therapy dogs as those who visit nursing homes and hospitals, providing comfort and companionship to those who need it. But therapy dogs fulfill a number of purposes within the health care setting in addition to visiting services. Two different types of therapy work have been distinguished, one called animal-assisted activities, which includes visiting services and group activities, and another called animal-assisted therapy, which involves using dogs to assist with patient treatment.

Animal-Assisted Activities

Animal-assisted activities can consist of visiting nursing home residents or hospital patients individually or providing group activities at these facilities. Group activities encourage interaction with the animal as well as discussion among the

A good therapy dog prospect is well socialized and enjoys human attention.

group. They may include demonstrations, informative lectures, or entertaining performances. Dogs who are trained in any advanced obedience discipline such as agility or freestyle can provide amazing demonstrations that stimulate communication, encourage participation, and generate smiles, all of which provide health benefits for the group participants.

Animal-Assisted Therapy

Animal-assisted therapy uses dogs or other animals as part of a formal treatment program. Dogs can be trained to perform various skills and activities to assist with physical, speech, or cognitive rehabilitation. Patients in physical rehabilitation can participate in games or activities with a dog that help improve range of motion, manual dexterity, and mobility. Brain-injured patients can benefit from various therapy-dog activities that help improve speech, memory, and other cognitive abilities.

Getting Started

Joining a local animal therapy organization is the best way to get started. These organizations can be instrumental in providing support, training, and resources for dog and handler teams. Providing listings of local and national organizations is a duty Therapy Dogs, Inc. has fulfilled quite admirably, with comprehensive information available at its website, www.therapydogs.com.

SHOWING YOUR POODLE

The AKC allows any registered purebred dog of at least six months of age to compete in conformation classes at AKC-sanctioned dog shows. Provided the particular dog show includes a class for Poodles, and your dog does not possess a fault that would disqualify him according to the breed standard, he is eligible to compete. Dog shows in Great Britain also require a dog to be at least six months old to enter.

Getting Started

Being eligible to compete does not necessarily mean your dog will do well in this sport. Getting involved in showing actually begins before you even acquire your dog, by studying the breed standard thoroughly and securing expert advice in choosing a good show prospect. The more you educate yourself before getting started, the better your chances are for success.

Breeders can advise you if they have any puppies who have show potential, but you should also seek advice from one other expert source before choosing a puppy. It is difficult to evaluate young puppies for show potential because their features are not developed enough to make an accurate determination, so don't be surprised if you need to purchase an older puppy if showing is your goal.

You can gain valuable insights about showing by attending dog shows and observing how they are organized and what kind of facilities they provide for grooming and preparation. They also have a schedule of show classes available, which will familiarize you with the types of classes and number of dogs typically entered in each class. Dog shows often host a selection of vendors that sell just about everything you need for showing, including specialty items that are difficult to find at typical pet supply stores. This is a good time to make a list of items you need and tally the costs involved.

Dog shows can also give you the opportunity to meet and talk to people involved in showing. You will find that most dog show exhibitors absolutely *love* to talk about their dogs and can be a great source of information and inspiration for those new to the sport. Those who are obviously busy preparing for a conformation class may be too preoccupied for conversation, but there are always good opportunities to approach people who have some down time between classes.

The more you educate yourself before participating in conformation, the better your chances for success.

Training Your Dog for Show

Show dogs require a good deal of training, just like dogs involved in any other type of canine sport. Socialization at a young age provides a crucial foundation for this training. Dog shows are noisy places, bustling with activity and an abundance of distractions, and dogs who have never been exposed to such an environment may become overwhelmed and stressed.

Training facilities and Poodle clubs offer training classes in conformation that will teach your dog the skills he needs to compete in dog shows. Your dog must learn how to stand for examination, move and turn on leash, and focus on his handler amid the distractions of noise and other dogs. As always, skills in basic obedience help prepare a dog for conformation training.

Conformation training classes are not just for the dog. You will need to learn how to move alongside your dog to show him to his best advantage. You need to learn how to fit and adjust a show choke collar, which is worn high on a show dog's neck just behind the ears. And you will need to master the fine art of leash handling. The end of your leash should never dangle haphazardly in a show ring. Experienced handlers often fold the excess leash up accordion-style so that it can be hidden inconspicuously in their hands, and the leash can then be lengthened if necessary by letting out a small section at a time. It takes practice to do this smoothly and efficiently.

You can combine this education with experience to turn yourself and your dog into a winning team. Participate in fun matches, which are dog shows that are not sanctioned by the AKC and do not provide points toward championships. However, they are great opportunities for novice exhibitors and young dogs to gain show experience. Take advantage of these opportunities to practice your skills and gain confidence.

Show dogs require a great deal of training.

Professional Handlers

Newcomers to the sport of showing may be apprehensive about handling their own dog, in which case professional handlers are available, for a fee, to show their dogs for them. If you are interested in hiring a professional handler, you should contact several handlers, review any agreements and fee schedules thoroughly, and observe the handlers at work before hiring. Breeders are often a good source for referrals.

Make sure you feel comfortable with the way the handler relates to your dog. Keep in mind that dogs and people are individuals. Your dog may not perform as well for a professional handler, because he may not be comfortable working with a stranger. Then again, some dogs respect and respond better to someone other than their owner. Many people who hire handlers eventually go on to show their own dogs after they have acquired the knowledge and confidence to do so.

What Is a Fun Match?

Fun matches are dog shows that are not sanctioned by the AKC and that do not provide points toward championships. They provide an opportunity for novice exhibitors and young dogs to gain show experience.

Show Grooming

Show grooming a Poodle takes a lot of skill, which can only be gained through practice and experience. If you are not proficient enough to produce a show-quality clip, hire someone to do the grooming for you. Professional handlers often provide grooming as a part of their service, but be prepared for additional expense. If you are interested in eventually grooming your own Poodle, you should be sure to observe the groomer at work to learn all the tricks of the trade.

Even if you hire someone to do the show clipping, you still must be instructed in the proper ways to maintain your Poodle's coat in between shows. Expert groomers are masters at disguising conformation faults, but they are not miracle workers. If your dog does not have a good-quality coat and sufficient hair length to work with, there is little a groomer can do to improve it.

Entering the Dog Show

Dog shows licensed by the KC are listed in the events section of their official publication, the *Kennel Gazette.* The AKC lists their sanctioned shows in a publication called the *AKC Gazette.* Schedules of dog shows also are published on the web sites of registries and breed clubs.

Once you find a show you want to participate in, complete an entry form and send it in with the required fees before the deadline. If you wait until a show is advertised to the public before deciding to enter, it may be too late to get your entry form in on time. Be sure to enter your dog in the correct class; different shows may offer different classes, so be sure you understand in which classes your dog is eligible to compete. (Dogs under a year old are usually entered in puppy classes.) A confirmation of your entry will be sent to you at least a week before the show.

The amount of time and expense you invest in showing depends entirely on the commitment you are willing to make. Some people show several times a month, while others are content to show a few times per year. Some may be motivated to achieve a championship, while others are happy to do it for fun and a few ribbons. If you attend only local shows, the costs will be considerably less than if you travel extensively to shows out of state.

Dressing for Success

Considering the work that goes into grooming a show dog, it makes sense that his ring partner should be just as well turned out. Men have traditionally worn coats and ties and women either skirts or dresses. Dress standards have loosened over the years to accept men in sport jackets and women in pantsuits, but the risk of facing a judge from the old school who may frown on casual dress is always a possibility. Larger, more prestigious dog shows obviously require the most respectful attire.

Whether you prefer formal or casual, conservative is key. Dog shows are not fashion shows, and you do not want to wear styles, colors, or patterns that direct attention away from your dog. Contrast or color coordination, however, can be used to set your dog off. A handler dressed in black can provide a good background for a white Poodle. A handler in navy blue looks great with a silver Poodle. Although men's suits do not have the color options of women's attire, it is always a good idea to pair dark-colored clothing with light-colored dogs and light-colored clothing with dark-colored dogs. A cream Poodle with a beige-suited handler does not make much of an impression on a judge and definitely creates a washed out picture at photo time.

Other tips to keep in mind revolve around function. Whatever you wear should have pockets. Pockets are handy for carrying the necessary dog treats to keep your dog's attention or to stow a small cloth for last minute cleanups, thus the popularity of jackets for men and women in the show ring. Shoes for either men or women should be comfortable and allow you to run smoothly alongside your dog. Most women opt for flat-soled shoes. Men should seek comfortable dress shoes or loafers. Always look for shoes that will provide good traction to prevent an embarrassing slip.

Judging

When it comes to a dog show, the judge is boss. She decides what will be done in what order, but she always requires three particular activities. The dog will be "stacked," that is, posed in a standing position for the judge's evaluation. The judge will inspect the dog at a distance and up close. She will also check the dog's teeth for proper alignment and possibly feel the body lightly to check conformation. (Judges are always careful not to dishevel a painstaking grooming.) In addition, she will want to view the dog's movement from the side. She will ask you to trot your dog past her, either individually or in a group with the rest of the class. And finally, she needs to observe the dog's movement from the front and behind by having the dog trot away from her and toward her. How often these activities are repeated and the pattern used by the exhibitors to trot their dogs is determined by the judge. The use of treats is usually permissible during any of these activities to keep the dog focused.

The classes are scheduled in a hierarchical system, beginning with dogs in the same breed, sex, and age categories competing against each other. The first-place winners of each class then go on to compete against the first-place winners from the other Poodle classes. Eventually, the top male and female Poodle will come head to head to determine the Best of Winners, who has the opportunity to compete against the top dogs of other breeds for the most prestigious of awards, the Best in Show.

So, how does your dog become a champion? The point system leading to a championship can be confusing, because the point scale varies depending on the breed and how many dogs are being judged in a class. A fair number of Poodles always attend dog shows, which results in stiffer competition. The AKC requires that a total of 15 points be earned to achieve a championship, with some of the points obtained from at least two major wins. A major win is one in which at least three points are gained.

Most judges attempt to be as fair as possible, but there is no denying that judges are individuals with different perspectives. Your dog may show well under one judge and not fare as well under another. This is par for the course. Regardless of how well your dog does in the show ring, there are many benefits to gain from the sport. You get to fraternize with other dog lovers and share your knowledge and experience with attendees who have an interest in your breed. Best of all, you get to show off your dog. So don't forget to smile and have *fun*! A positive attitude is what makes a true winner.

Dog shows evaluate a dog as he compares to the breed standard.

Advanced Obedience Training

The goal of advanced obedience training is to improve a dog's performance of basic obedience skills and develop some additional skills needed for a number of advanced activities.

OBEDIENCE

Poodles enjoy obedience work immensely. It exercises their active minds and bodies by giving them a job to do, and it helps appease their seemingly insatiable appetite for human attention. Poodles have done very well in obedience competition, and it is a very rewarding activity for Poodle owners who seek to enjoy the many benefits associated with having a well-trained dog.

For those interested in obedience competition, you must locate an advanced training program specifically designed to train the skills required for this sport. Additional skills needed for obedience competition include retrieving, directed jumping, drop-on-recall, scent discrimination, coming to heel, and hand signals. Very often, the format for these classes is flexible, depending on the particular needs of the class participants. Because this type of competition involves different levels, opportunities are available to advance to additional titles as your dog acquires more skills and becomes more proficient.

The Novice level in AKC-sanctioned obedience trials requires your dog to demonstrate the skills required of a good canine companion and will earn your dog the Companion Dog (CD) title. Necessary skills include coming when called, staying with a group of dogs, standing for examination, and heeling on and off leash.

The Open level takes training a little further and results in a Companion Dog Excellent (CDX) title. In addition to performing the Novice exercises off leash, Open level dogs are required to execute some skills for longer periods of time and accomplish a number of new skills, such as retrieving and jumping. To reach this level, it is important to find a training class that covers retrieving, jumping, out-of-sight stays, and drop-on-recall.

The Utility level involves the most difficult exercises in obedience competition, including such skills as directed jumping and directed retrieving. Those who excel at this level attain the respected Utility Dog (UD) title. The most interesting skill to observe at this level is scent discrimination, where the dog must retrieve an object bearing his owner's scent from a group of other objects. Again, those wishing to succeed at this level must enroll in the appropriate training class to practice these skills.

Obedience competition need not end at a UD title. Those who have achieved a UD can continue to compete at the Utility level and work toward a Utility Dog Excellent (UDX) title. They can also earn points to gain the title of Obedience Trial Champion (OTCh.). The progressive levels in obedience competition provide opportunities for dog owners to get involved at an early stage of training while providing incentives and goals for advancement. The requirements of the sport are only as demanding as the dog owner's drive to succeed.

COMPETITIVE SPORTS

Agility

The heart-pounding, adrenaline-packed sport of dog agility has become one of the most popular dog sports in North America and Europe. It began in Great Britain as an exhibition sport and had already caught the attention of dog trainers in the United States by the time it made its debut at the Crufts Dog Show in 1979. The speed, colorful obstacles, and athletic challenges presented by agility appeal to competitors and spectators alike.

The sport involves a course of obstacles through which a dog must negotiate at the direction of his handler. Dogs who complete the course fastest, without errors, are awarded. The obstacles include a number of interesting configurations, including jumps that are constructed in single and double formations similar to those found in grand prix equestrian events.

A number of national organizations sanction agility trials in the United States, including the AKC, United Kennel Club (UKC), United States Dog Agility Association (USDAA), North American Dog

Heeling on leash is a necessary skill for competing in obedience.

Agility Council (NADAC), and Canine Performance Events (CPE). In Great Britain, all dog agility events are governed by the KC. Some trials conform to international rules, which require the highest level of speed and skill, and others are domestic competitions that do not require quite as much physical ability.

Agility is an excellent sport for Toy and Miniature Poodles due to their athletic abilities and energetic drive. The agility course is a canine playground for these active little dogs. It is also one of the best confidence-building sports for shy or timid dogs. Even the Toy Poodle, whose size seems to present a barrier, can participate by adjusting the equipment and lowering the jumps. The Teacup Dogs Agility Association (TDAA) is an organization that promotes agility for diminutive breeds by using scaled-down versions of agility equipment appropriate for small dogs less than 17 inches (43.2 cm) in height.

This type of dog sport does require a considerable amount of commitment and training to become proficient, and joining a local agility club or taking training classes is necessary to reach a competitive level. It also takes some physical effort from the handlers, as they need to run through the course with their dogs in order to direct their dogs to the appropriate obstacles. Because the layout of obstacle courses and the order in which obstacles must be surmounted is different for each event, it takes an alert handler and an attentive dog to be successful.

Agility need not be limited to those with lofty goals, though. For many, dog agility is a fun pastime, a way to spend time with and exercise their dogs in a positive way.

Flyball

Flyball is another fast-paced, exciting canine sport that involves races between teams of dogs. Each team consists of four dogs who run a 51-foot (15.5-m) course in relay fashion. Four jumps are placed along the course, with a flyball box at the end. A dog runs the length of the course and presses a pedal on the front of the flyball box to activate the release of a ball. The dog then retrieves the ball and races back down the jump course to the finish/start line, where the next dog on the team is released to run the course. The team whose dogs complete the course fastest, without missing jumps or dropping balls, wins.

Dogs who have a high energy level and love to fetch balls make excellent candidates for flyball competition. Poodles, being athletic jumpers with an abundance of energy and a love for ball play, have a natural aptitude for this sport. Even the tiny Toy Poodle is not excluded from participation, because jump heights are adjusted according to the size of the smallest dog on the team.

Getting started in this activity involves enrolling in a flyball training program, available at many dog training facilities, or joining a local flyball club. The North American Flyball Association, Inc.'s website at www.flyball.org provides a database of flyball clubs for those seeking a club in their area.

Sports and Safety

Canine sports, like human sports, involve some risk of physical injury. Taking steps to avoid accidents allows you and your dog to continue enjoying the many benefits of canine activities. The following precautions should be observed while practicing or competing in any canine sport:

1. Always check your training and sport equipment prior to practice or competition to make sure everything is in good repair and operating correctly. This includes jumps, obstacles, and even collars and leashes.

2. Keep your dog in good physical shape with regular practice and exercise. Do not encourage your dog to overexert himself, even if he seems to have the will and drive to work indefinitely.

3. Postpone or cancel practices or competitions if your dog displays any signs of soreness or illness. If your dog is not in top condition, he will be more prone to injuries. Health conditions may worsen, or he may spread illness to other dogs.

4. Always bring a canine first-aid kit with you to any canine sport event.

5. Seek veterinary attention immediately if your dog is injured while practicing or competing. Treating injuries professionally and promptly will get your dog back in top form quickly, while ignoring injuries may result in permanent damage that will exclude your dog from future competition.

Freestyle

Canine musical freestyle is a new

sport that has exploded on the dog scene in recent years. It continues to rise in popularity across the nation and the world. It is a unique blend of dog obedience, trick training, dance, and music, all of which contribute to an exciting display of teamwork between dog and handler. Costumes and musical interpretation add color to the routines and contribute to the lively spirit of freestyle competitions. Its phenomenal growth is not so surprising, since freestyle adds excitement and rhythm to an otherwise stuffy obedience competition. It has given obedience competitors a new and thrilling option to consider.

Often referred to as "dog dancing," freestyle routines include traditional obedience skills with the addition of unique maneuvers such as sidestepping, leg weaving, and spins to create a dance-like performance to music. The Poodle's agility and intelligence make him exceptionally suited to this sport. It is not hard to convince a Poodle to become a teammate with his handler, and his lively personality is sure to add pizzazz to any performance. If there is one thing a Poodle loves to do, it is entertain. In fact, the history of musical freestyle is sometimes

traced as far back as the performing dogs of an earlier era, when circuses employed Poodles in musical performances. A favored performer in bygone days, the Poodle continues to have a high aptitude for such work.

The two most influential organizations in the United Kingdom are Canine Freestyle GB and Paws N Music Association. In the United States, the Canine Freestyle Federation (CFF),

Rewarding your dog for a job well done will strengthen the bond between the two of you.

World Canine Freestyle Organization (WCFO), Paws2Dance, and Musical Dog Sport Association (MDSA) have established themselves as authorities. Those interested in participating should find out which organizations sponsor competitions in their area and which format is taught at local training facilities.

Playing with your dog will help keep him happy and healthy.

Attending a freestyle event may be the best way to see what is involved in freestyle competition and decide if it is something that interests you. But don't be surprised if you experience rather large crowds, because freestyle is still a novelty at canine events and tends to attract many curious spectators. To learn more about this fun and innovative sport, check out the websites for CFF at www.canine-freestyle.org or the WCFO at www.worldcaninefreestyle.org.

Advanced training in any pursuit is always time well spent. You and your Poodle can learn so much about each other and develop a bond stronger than you may have thought possible. When you and your dog learn to understand each other through training, you also learn to appreciate, respect, and trust each other. Can there be any better relationship than this?

Everyday Sports

Getting off the couch to spend time with our dogs keeps us active and provides social opportunities, nurturing both our physical and emotional well-being.

- **Dog Walking:** This is a low-impact activity that does not damage joints or overexert muscles, and it can provide moderate aerobic benefits, depending on the briskness of your speed. Few dogs would pass up the opportunity to join you for walks, which makes it a mutually enjoyable experience.

- **Jogging and Cycling:** Toy and Miniature Poodles, being of smaller stature, expend a lot of energy to cover distance and are not known to have the endurance of larger, long-legged breeds. While Miniature Poodles are capable of joining their owners on shorter, leisurely jogs, the Toy Poodle would probably politely decline the rigors on his tiny body.

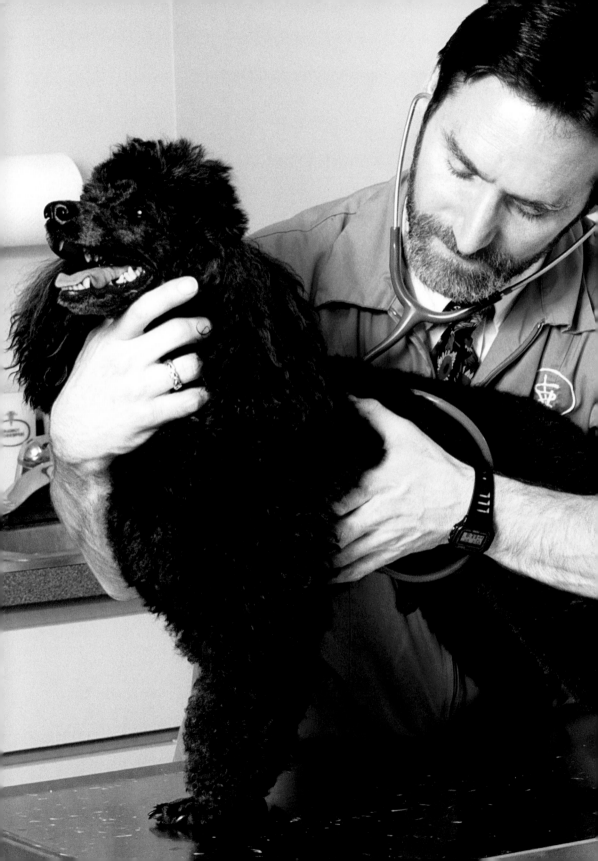

8

HEALTH

of Your Toy or Miniature Poodle

Toy and Miniature Poodles have a longer-than-average lifespan in canine terms, and most of us would not want to part with them a moment sooner. They are our source of joy and comfort, our constant companions, and valued members of our families. It is our responsibility and duty to provide them with the very best care to ensure their health and safety. Fortunately, a health maintenance routine, prompt veterinary care, and emergency preparedness can help keep your Toy or Miniature Poodle hopping happily into his senior years.

FINDING A VETERINARIAN

Your veterinarian is the most important link to your dog's health and quality of life. She will provide health maintenance services, expert advice, and emergency care that can prolong the life and comfort of your pet. In other words, your dog's life will be in her hands. This is why it is important to choose a veterinarian as carefully as you would your own doctor.

Asking for Referrals

If you do not already have a veterinarian with whom you feel comfortable, the best way to locate one is through referrals from friends, relatives, or co-workers. Be sure to ask these people what they like about their veterinarians and what kinds of services they have received in the past. Other good sources for referrals include Poodle breeders and Poodle rescue organizations. While most veterinarians have plenty of experience with dogs, finding a veterinarian with experience handling the specific health conditions associated with a particular breed has its advantages.

Making the Call

Whether you obtain a referral for a veterinarian or locate one in the telephone book, a phone call to the vet's office for further questioning will help you make important determinations. Ask the staff what kind of special equipment they have. Modern

Annual veterinary exams should be an integral part of your pet-care routine.

anesthetic equipment, such as isofluorothane anesthesia, is desirable because it is safer and provides quicker anesthetic recovery. If the clinic boasts its own ultrasound, x-ray, and laboratory test equipment, it will save you the time and expense of being referred to another clinic or laboratory for these services.

The First Visit

When you have located a veterinarian, your first visit should involve further evaluation. Observe how organized and professional the office staff appears to be, how well the animals are treated, and whether the exam rooms are kept clean. Your dog's first examination should be thorough, and the veterinarian should take the time to answer your questions and address your concerns without rushing to get to the next client.

On occasion, every veterinary clinic experiences an inordinate number of emergency cases to handle, which result in longer waits and delays in service. Patience is always a good quality to take with you to the vet's office. Just remember that when your own pet needs immediate attention in an emergency, you will be thankful for your vet's prompt response and the understanding of the other patrons.

ANNUAL PHYSICAL EXAMINATIONS

Annual veterinary exams should be an integral part of your pet-care routine. It is always easier to prevent problems than treat them. Your veterinarian may notice slight changes in your dog's health that may have occurred so gradually they escaped your attention. This is also a good time to get professional advice on behavior or health issues you have encountered.

The physical examination involves inspecting your dog from nose to tail. The nose will be checked for discharge, the eyes will be checked for signs of illness or sight impairment, and the ears will be checked for redness, swelling, or infection. The mouth can give a number of clues to the general health of a dog as well. Oral problems are often the source of infections or weight loss, and the gums can indicate anemic or circulatory conditions.

Your veterinarian will also check the skin and coat, which can reveal problems with parasites, allergies, hereditary diseases, or general health. She will palpate the abdomen to detect any tumors or internal problems and will be alert to any signs of discomfort or pain during the examination. Finally, she will check the heart and lungs to detect any cardiovascular problems.

Although a physical exam can detect external parasites, it cannot detect internal parasites. Your veterinarian may recommend a blood test to check for heartworm and a fecal analysis to check for intestinal parasites.

The Annual Exam

Annual physical veterinary exams should be an integral part of your pet-care routine, one reason being that your vet may notice slight changes in your dog's health that have escaped your attention.

VACCINATIONS

The annual checkup provides an opportunity to update vaccinations. Dogs are required by law to be vaccinated against rabies every one to three years, depending on your state of residence. Other vaccines are optional but can provide important protection against a number of serious diseases. Many vaccines are combined, so you do not need to get a separate inoculation for each disease.

Canine Distemper

Canine distemper is a virus that affects the nervous system and internal organs. Spread by contact with an infected dog's secretions, unprotected dogs are at high risk of contracting this virus. It is fatal for 50 percent of dogs and 75 percent of puppies. Initial symptoms include discharge from the eyes and nose, listlessness, fever, coughing, diarrhea, and vomiting. In the later stages, it may result in convulsions, paralysis, and death. As is the case with most viruses, no cure is available, and treatment is limited to supportive care. Drugs can help minimize the symptoms of nausea, vomiting, diarrhea, and convulsions, and intravenous fluids help combat dehydration. Antibiotics may be necessary to treat secondary infections, such as pneumonia. Even with successful treatment, survivors are often plagued with continuing health problems caused by permanent damage to the nervous system.

Canine Parvovirus

Canine parvovirus is a highly contagious virus that primarily affects a dog's gastrointestinal system but can also affect the heart. Spread through the feces of infected animals, it can cause high fevers, listlessness, bloody diarrhea, and vomiting. Severe cases are most often fatal for puppies, and adult dogs have a 50 percent chance of survival. Treatment may consist of administering intravenous fluids and medications for vomiting. However, dogs who survive may experience residual heart problems that can eventually lead to congestive heart failure.

Parainfluenza

Parainfluenza is a virus that causes a mild respiratory tract infection, with symptoms of coughing and nasal discharge. It is spread through contact with nasal secretions or airborne particles and is highly contagious in situations where many dogs come in contact with each other, such as kennels, shelters, and dog shows. Although most cases resolve on their own, parainfluenza does stress the immune system and makes dogs susceptible to serious secondary infections, such as pneumonia. Treatment is usually not necessary for a mild form of the disease, but infected dogs should be isolated from other dogs and monitored for more serious symptoms. Secondary infections must be treated with antibiotics.

Parainfluenza is highly contagious in situations where dogs come into contact with one another.

Canine Coronavirus

Canine coronavirus is a disease that causes gastrointestinal problems, with symptoms of diarrhea, vomiting, lack of appetite, listlessness, dehydration, and depression. It is spread through the ingestion of feces and can be very severe, even fatal, for puppies. Treatment is limited to relieving symptoms using antidiarrheals and antivomiting drugs and replacing lost fluids to prevent dehydration.

Canine Adenovirus-1

Canine adenovirus-1 (infectious canine hepatitis) is a virus that affects the dog's liver and spreads through contact with an infected dog's urine, feces, and saliva. Symptoms include vomiting, jaundice, lack of appetite, and stomach enlargement. The effects of this virus can range from very mild to fatal. Treatment may consist of intravenous fluids to help prevent dehydration and supplementation with vitamins and amino acids to help minimize the effects on the liver. A separate vaccine for this virus is not necessary, because the canine adenovirus-2 vaccine provides protection.

Canine Adenovirus-2

Canine adenovirus-2 is often seen in combination with other viruses. It causes upper respiratory infections that produce a dry, hacking cough. Although not usually serious, it can cause significant problems for older dogs or those with weakened immune systems.

Leptospirosis

Leptospirosis is caused by bacteria that target a dog's liver and kidneys, sometimes resulting in liver disease and kidney failure. Infection occurs after contact with the urine of infected animals and can result in symptoms of fever, jaundice, loss of appetite, internal bleeding, and excessive consumption of water. Antibiotic therapy has been known to reduce the duration of the disease, which in turn minimizes the damage to liver and kidneys. Additional supportive treatment may be necessary to compensate for reduced liver and kidney functions, and severe cases may require blood transfusions. Infected dogs may remain contagious for up to three months following treatment of the active form of the disease, and because this disease poses a risk of contagion to humans as well as other animals, infected dogs should be quarantined and contaminated areas kept disinfected.

Bordetella (Kennel Cough)

Bordetella (kennel cough) is characterized by a severe chronic cough caused by a respiratory bacterium. It is spread easily among dogs through coughing and sneezing, which is why it tends to surface in places where dogs congregate, such as kennels and dog shows. It is seldom fatal, but vaccination is recommended for dogs who are at a high risk of being exposed to the bacteria. Treatment is limited to symptomatic relief through the use of prescription or nonprescription cough suppressants. Secondary bacterial infections may need to be treated with antibiotics.

Lyme Disease

Lyme disease (*Borrelia burgdorferi*) is a bacterial disease that is transmitted by infected ticks. Symptoms of infection include loss of appetite, listlessness, fever, acute arthritis, lameness, and swelling around the site of the tick bite. Risk of contracting this disease is limited to areas where infected ticks exist. Dogs who live in these areas should be vaccinated before tick season. If a dog becomes infected, treatment with the antibiotic tetracycline is usually prescribed.

Inspect your Poodle for ticks after he's been playing outside.

Rabies

Rabies is a very serious virus that affects the nervous system and ultimately results in death. The symptoms provide the essential elements of a horror movie. Infected animals become vicious, incoherent, and unpredictable. They may froth at the mouth, suffer from vocal paralysis, and appear to be oblivious to pain. It is easily transmitted through the body fluids of an infected animal and poses a serious risk to humans. Due to the severe consequences of this virus and the fact that there is no cure, rabies vaccinations for dogs are required by law.

ALTERING YOUR DOG

If you will not be showing or breeding your Toy or Miniature Poodle, you should have him altered. This prevents your dog from contributing to the overwhelming problem of pet overpopulation while providing many benefits for the two of you. For you, altering will eliminate hormone-driven canine behaviors that can be challenging to manage, such as roaming and marking territory (urinating in the house). For your dog, there are a number of health benefits to consider. Sterilized dogs are not prone to certain diseases, tumors, or complications associated with the reproductive organs, which means they have a better chance of living longer, healthier lives.

Castration involves removing the testicles of a male dog. The dog is placed under anesthesia, and an incision is made in front of the scrotum. The testicles are then removed, and the vas deferens (spermatic cord) is tied off, along with the vessels that provide blood supply. The incision may be closed with absorbable sutures, removable sutures, or staples, depending on the veterinarian's choice.

Spaying, also called *ovariohysterectomy*, consists of surgically removing both ovaries and the uterus of a female dog. Because this operation involves entering the abdomen, it is considered major surgery and is obviously more complicated and invasive than castration. After the dog is anesthetized, a small incision is made in the belly, and the reproductive organs are removed. Blood vessels are tied off, and the incision is closed with absorbable sutures, removable sutures, or staples.

Dogs under anesthesia feel no pain during these procedures, and the soreness afterward dissipates quickly. Your dog may be lethargic after surgery due to the effects of anesthesia and sedation, but in most cases, he or she will be back to normal within a few days. Females may take a little longer to recover due to the complexity of spaying, but they still have a very quick recovery rate.

Postoperative care for males and females is minimal. Dog

owners should watch for any redness or discharge from the incision site and prevent their dogs from licking this area excessively. The most difficult aspect of postoperative care involves keeping the dog quiet and minimizing activity for two weeks following surgery. Overexertion can result in complications, but high-energy dogs like Toy and Miniature Poodles do not always have a low gear!

Dogs can be altered as young as eight weeks old, but many veterinarians still prefer to wait until a dog is at least five months old. Complications from surgery are rare, but many veterinarians now recognize the importance of preanesthesia screening. Some risks are associated with any surgery requiring the use of anesthesia, and dogs who have pre-existing problems, such as reduced kidney or liver function, face a greater risk. Your vet may recommend a blood test to rule out potential problems that cannot be detected by a physical examination prior to surgery.

Recognizing that dogs do experience some pain and discomfort after surgery, some veterinarians now prescribe pain medication for postoperative use. However, you should consider the fact that a little pain is sometimes a good thing. It is difficult enough to prevent an active dog from overexerting himself after surgery without eliminating the pain.

EXTERNAL PARASITES

Parasites are small animals that live on or in animals of other species. They obtain at least part of their sustenance from their

Altering your Poodle will eliminate hormone-driven canine behaviors, such as roaming.

animal host but provide nothing to their host in return. On the contrary, they can drain valuable resources from a dog's body to such a degree that a dog's health can become seriously compromised.

External parasites are those that live on the surface of their host, clinging to hair, crawling on skin, or burrowing into the skin. They are the most common cause of skin irritations for pets, and they are a great source of distress for both pets and their owners.

Fleas

Fleas are tiny, blood-sucking insects that cause more frustration for dog owners than any other parasite. They are prolific breeders, with females producing up to 2,000 eggs in a few weeks, so a mild case of fleas can become a severe problem in a short time. Fleas can be a particular nuisance in warmer climates, where the flea season lasts most of the year. But even in northern climates, the 7-month flea season does not prevent fleas from continuing to breed within the warm environment of a home during the winter months.

Does My Dog Have Fleas?

Scratching and biting are two of the most obvious signs that your dog has fleas. You can also part his hair and look for reddish-brown insects on his skin. In addition, check for flea dirt, which consists of flea droppings that look like tiny black flecks of dirt.

Symptoms

Aside from the obvious scratching and biting, you can tell if your dog has fleas by parting the hair and looking for the reddish-brown insects scurrying along the skin. Another sign of flea infestation is the flea dirt they leave behind. Flea dirt consists of flea droppings that look like tiny black flecks of dirt. Because flea dirt is comprised of digested blood, it turns a reddish color when reconstituted with water. A heavily infested dog will turn pinkish-red when he is bathed.

Fleas can cause a number of problems for dogs aside from a persistent and annoying itch. Skin irritation can become quite severe, especially for dogs who develop sensitivity to flea saliva. Flea allergy dermatitis causes intense scratching, loss of hair, and skin damage that can lead to bacterial infections. In some cases, fleas can consume enough blood to cause life-threatening anemia. Puppies are particularly prone to losing too much blood, because they do not have the blood volume of an adult dog.

Treatment and Prevention

The biggest challenge in getting rid of a flea problem is that the adult fleas, which are the little creatures you see on your dog, only constitute 5 percent of the flea life cycle. The other 95 percent of fleas are in various stages of development, including eggs, larvae, and pupae. Fleas lay their eggs throughout the house, particularly in carpeting along the base of furniture and along the walls. They also deposit eggs in shaded areas outdoors, especially where your dog likes to spend time. Because the immature stages of fleas are immune to the effects of pesticides, killing the adult fleas does little to eradicate these bothersome pests.

To be effective, the battle against fleas must be fought on several fronts. First, the fleas must be removed from all animals in the home. A great variety of flea products is available at pet supply stores, and these are adequate for the job. Flea dips and shampoos are quite effective in killing adult fleas, and some of them provide residual benefits as well. Because these items are applied during a bath, this is a good opportunity to check the condition of the skin and wash flea dirt out of the coat. Powders and sprays are a bit messy to apply, but you may want to use them if bathing is not practical.

Next, the home and yard should be treated. The home should be thoroughly vacuumed, especially along baseboards and furniture. Areas where your dog likes to lay should be vacuumed, cleaned, or washed. This includes his dog bed, furniture cushions, and crate. Sprays or indoor foggers can then be used to kill the insects that remain hidden throughout the home. Outdoor sprays are used to treat those outdoor areas at risk of harboring fleas and their eggs.

After eradicating the fleas from your household pets, home, and yard, retreatment is necessary to kill the rest of the fleas emerging from egg or pupae stages. Make sure that you read and adhere to the instructions on any flea control product and retreat areas according to the timetable given.

Finally, preventatives can be used to reduce the chance of recurrence. Flea collars and topical spot-on treatments are popular products to prevent reinfestation. To prevent adverse reactions, these items should be used strictly according to manufacturer recommendations.

Ticks

Ticks are small, blood-sucking parasites that are responsible for transmitting a number of diseases to animals and people. The most common concerns for companion dogs are Lyme disease, ehrlichiosis, and tick paralysis. Lyme disease can result in a number of serious symptoms, such as lameness, swollen joints, fever, and fatigue. Ehrlichiosis causes high fevers, anemia, lethargy, and muscle aches, while tick paralysis progressively affects coordination and can result in paralysis of the rear legs.

Ticks use their spidery legs to grab onto a host as it passes by. They then seek a warm, vulnerable spot to bury their tiny heads into the skin for a blood meal. On dogs, they prefer the thin, blood-rich skin of the ears and also tend to inhabit other areas of the head and neck. Their barbed mouths attach themselves quite firmly to their hosts, and their hard, flat bodies are difficult to detect and impervious to being crushed. Many times, ticks are not noticeable until they have become engorged with blood.

Several species of these small, crab-like creatures are found throughout North America. All of them like to reside in tall grasses or under fallen leaves in wooded or shaded areas. Precautions should be taken in areas where the risk of disease transmission is high. Vaccinations for Lyme disease are recommended for dogs who live where the disease is prevalent, especially for dogs who spend a lot of time outdoors in wooded or grassy areas. Dog owners should examine their dogs daily and remove ticks immediately. Sometimes it takes hours for a tick to transmit a disease, so the sooner the tick is removed, the better. Other precautions include keeping grass mowed, stacking firewood off the ground and away from the house, and using tick-killing pesticides. Contact your veterinarian for advice on what product is best for your dog.

Keeping Ticks Out of Your Yard

To keep ticks out of your yard, keep the grass mowed, stack firewood off the ground and away from the house, and use tick-killing pesticides.

How to Remove a Tick

To remove a tick, use tweezers to grasp the tick close to the skin, and pull it off gently. If you use your fingers to remove a tick, you may increase the chance of transmitting disease by squeezing the infectious material into your dog. Afterward, clean the bite site, tweezers, and your hands with disinfectant. If you suspect your dog may have contracted a tick-borne disease, seek veterinary attention immediately. Lyme disease is most successfully treated with antibiotics if it is diagnosed early.

Mites

Mites are tiny creatures that resemble microscopic ticks. Several species can cause problems for dogs, including ear mites, sarcoptic mites, and demodex mites.

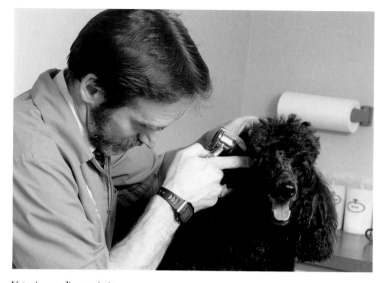

Veterinary diagnosis is needed to determine whether your Poodle is suffering from ear mites.

Ear Mites

Ear mites most commonly affect cats but can also cause problems for dogs. They are easily transmitted via physical contact with an infected host, so all dogs and cats in the home must be treated if one of them is infected. Ear mites live on the surface of the ear canal and sometimes on the head or other parts of the body. They feast on earwax and skin oils and cause a black ear discharge that is comprised of earwax, blood, and mites. They also cause ear inflammation and can contribute to secondary yeast or bacterial infections.

Some dogs are sensitive to ear mites and will engage in head shaking and ear scratching, causing further damage to the ears. Because dogs are prone to ear infections from a number of sources, veterinary diagnosis is needed to confirm that ear mites are the culprit. Treatment is effective using a number of products that your veterinarian can prescribe.

Sarcoptic Mites

Sarcoptic mites are responsible for causing the condition known as mange, or scabies. These little pests burrow into the skin and cause inflammation, severe itching, and hair loss. Scratching causes further damage in the form of crusty skin lesions, scabs, and additional hair loss. These symptoms mimic those of an allergic dermatitis and contribute to the incidence of misdiagnosis.

Sarcoptic mites are highly contagious and sometimes difficult to diagnose. Skin scrapings do not always reveal their presence, and scrapings may have to be repeated until the mites are found. To make things worse, scabies can be transmitted to humans. Although these mites are not known to reproduce very readily on a healthy human, they can cause problems for those with suppressed immunity.

Treatment may consist of special insecticide dips or sprays prescribed by your veterinarian in addition to diet supplementation to help rejuvenate damaged skin. Ivermectin, a prescription insecticide available in injection form, has also been used successfully to treat this problem, although it is not yet approved for this use. Your veterinarian can prescribe a comprehensive treatment program to get these frustrating pests under control.

Demodex Mites

Demodex mites cause a type of mange referred to as *demodectic mange* or *red mange*. These little critters are not considered as serious a problem as sarcoptic mites because they exist naturally on a dog's skin and do not cause problems for most dogs. But when their population bursts out of control, symptoms of hair loss, itching, and skin lesions become apparent. Secondary infections may cause inflammation and reddened skin—thus the origin of the name *red mange*.

Demodex mites live within the hair follicles and are easier to detect in skin scrapings than are sarcoptic mites. Symptoms are usually localized to a particular part of the body and result in patches of hair loss, most often found on the head or legs. When the condition spreads to affect large areas of the body, it is called *generalized demodicosis* and becomes much more difficult to bring under control.

Because a dog's immune system keeps the population of demodex mites in check, dogs with immature or weakened immune systems are most prone to developing problems. Demodectic mange commonly affects young dogs under the age of two due to a lack of immunity that is thought to be hereditary. In most cases, it can be treated the same as a sarcoptic mite infection, with dips, sprays, and other treatments prescribed by your veterinarian. For young dogs, mild forms of affliction may regress without treatment as the dog's immune system matures.

More than 90 percent of puppies are infected with worms, mainly because several worm species are transmitted to puppies from their mothers before they are born or through the mother's milk. Untreated dogs and puppies contaminate soil with the worm eggs in their feces, and the eggs are then tracked into our homes. Worms are not only a health concern for canines—they can also infect humans. It is estimated that 5 to 20 percent of children have been infected with roundworms at some time. Thus, it is important to worm puppies and check the stools of adult dogs annually.

For older dogs, the underlying cause of suppressed immunity must be addressed before treatment will be successful.

INTERNAL PARASITES

Internal parasites are small animals that live inside a dog's body, specifically within the digestive and circulatory systems. Within this warm and protected environment, they can feed, grow, and eventually produce eggs or larvae that leave the dog's body to infect other hosts. Controlling internal parasites is a priority, because they can overburden a dog's body to cause severe symptoms or even death. They can also spread to other animals, and in some cases, to humans.

Intestinal Worms

Several intestinal parasites can cause problems for dogs, all of which are classified as worms. Some are large enough to be seen with the naked eye, while others must be diagnosed by examining stool samples under a microscope. Magnification helps detect the worm eggs and determine which species is the culprit.

Roundworms

Roundworms thrive in the intestine, where they can grow 5 (12.7 cm) to 7 inches (17.8 cm) long. Dogs become infected by ingesting roundworm eggs found in feces or contaminated soil. The eggs hatch in the intestines, and the larvae are subsequently transported to the lungs through the bloodstream. The larvae then crawl up the windpipe, where they are swallowed by the dog and develop into adults when they return to the intestines.

Roundworms are most often a problem for puppies. Although they do not usually cause problems for adult dogs, the larvae may become encysted in the body tissue of a female dog and become active in the later stages of pregnancy. They are then transmitted to puppies while in utero or through the mother's milk. Encysted larvae are immune to treatment, so treating the adult dog will not prevent transmission of these parasites from a mother dog to her puppies. For this reason, it is important for all puppies to receive worming treatments.

Roundworm infestations in puppies may result in poor growth, lack of appetite, lack of energy, diarrhea, vomiting, and the appearance of a bloated belly. In severe cases, roundworms can cause an intestinal obstruction, resulting in death. These pests are easily eliminated with proper worming treatments that your veterinarian can prescribe. But as with other parasitic pests, treatment is only effective in eliminating the adult stage of the worm. Subsequent treatments are necessary to eradicate any adult worms that develop from the surviving larvae.

Hookworms

Hookworms get their name from the hook-like teeth they use to adhere to the intestinal wall. Like roundworms, they are intestinal parasites that are ingested by dogs when they come in contact with egg-bearing stools or contaminated soil. They are also transmitted from pregnant females to their offspring through uterine migration or the mother's milk. This type of worm has an additional mode of infection, because the larvae are capable of burrowing directly through the dog's skin.

These small, thin worms, which can only be detected by magnification, subsist on a diet of blood and result in symptoms such as diarrhea (sometimes bloody), anemia, inability to thrive, and lack of energy. Puppies can be severely affected by the loss of blood, which can harm their growth and possibly result in death. Treatment is the same as for roundworms.

Whipworms

Whipworms are so named because of their long, thread-like tails. They can only infect a dog through consumption of their eggs, which are found in feces or contaminated soil. Whipworms prefer to reside in a dog's large intestine, where they imbed their long tails into the intestinal wall. They can be difficult to detect because they do not shed large amounts of eggs, and they do not always cause symptoms. When symptoms do occur, they may include anemia, dehydration, diarrhea, and weight loss. Several fecal examinations may be necessary to detect whipworms, but they are easily eliminated using proper worming treatments.

Tapeworms

Tapeworms are long, flat, segmented worms that live within the intestine. They attach to the intestinal wall with hooks located on their heads, and they absorb food through their skin. Although infected dogs do not always display symptoms, severe infestation

Types of Intestinal Worms

The following intestinal worms can cause major problems for dogs:

roundworms

hookworms

whipworms

tapeworms

heartworms

may result in abdominal discomfort, vomiting, or weight loss. The most obvious signs of tapeworm infection are severe itching around the anus and the appearance of tapeworm segments near the rectum.

Tapeworms shed the tail-end segments of their bodies, which are excreted by the dog and appear in the feces or become stuck to the hair and skin around the anus. These body parts are actually egg casings that release hundreds of eggs once they are dry. They resemble rectangular pieces of confetti and move with slow, worm-like undulations until they dry and harden.

Tapeworms are most frequently transmitted by fleas. Fleas consume tapeworm eggs, which hatch and begin to develop within

Puppies can be severely affected by internal parasites.

the fleas. When a dog consumes the fleas by licking or biting itchy areas, the tapeworm has the opportunity to develop into the adult stage in the dog's intestine. The best preventive against tapeworms is to keep fleas at bay. Infected dogs must be treated with the appropriate veterinarian-recommended worming medication, because wormers used to eliminate other intestinal worms are not effective against tapeworms.

Heartworms

Heartworm has become one of the greatest concerns in canine health because of its broad spread throughout the United States and other countries. Many veterinarians, along with national and international groups, have initiated campaigns promoting heartworm prevention.

Why all the fuss? Because heartworm is a death sentence for untreated dogs. Even if treatment is afforded, an infected dog must go through a lengthy and uncomfortable treatment process, and the outcome is questionable, depending on the extent of infection and the damage to vital organs. Prevention is the best way to address this problem, and pharmaceutical companies continue to develop newer, easier ways to do this.

Heartworms, like other parasites, go through several life stages before developing into adults. The larvae circulate through their host's bloodstream until ingested by a mosquito. They undergo further development within the mosquito until they are ready to infect a new host, which is accomplished when the mosquito bites another dog. The larvae then develop within the new host to become the long, spaghetti-like worms that congregate in a dog's heart. The adult worms can grow 10 (25.4 cm) to 14 inches (35.6 cm) long, and the females produce thousands of live larvae per day that course through the animal's bloodstream. These larvae, called *microfilariae*, are the beginning of a new generation awaiting assistance from its intermediate host, the mosquito.

It may take six to seven months after the initial infection before adult worms begin to reproduce, and symptoms in the dog may not appear for several years. When the heart and its surrounding blood vessels become overburdened with heartworms, dogs begin to show decreased energy and stamina, as well as weight loss. Worms can also infest the arteries to the lungs and cause coughing and difficulty breathing. If they become lodged in the veins of the liver, they can cause reduced liver or kidney function. These symptoms become progressively worse as the heartworms continue to invade the dog's body.

Blood tests are available to detect infection of either the microfilariae in the blood or the adult worms in the heart. The adult worms can also be detected by radiograph (x-ray), and additional tests can determine the effect on heart, kidney, and liver function prior to treatment.

Treatment involves the use of medications to kill the worms, but success often depends on the severity of the infection. Dogs whose systems have already been greatly compromised by heartworms may have difficulty tolerating the treatment. The drug used to kill heartworms contains arsenic, and dogs with distressed livers and kidneys may have difficulty breaking down and eliminating this poison. In very advanced cases of heartworm, there is little a veterinarian can do to prolong the life of the dog. The

Did You Know?

Purebred dogs are often inbred to establish consistent characteristics in the breed, but inbreeding can also increase the risk of inheriting genetic defects.

worms, once killed, must be absorbed by the dog's body, which presents the additional risk that one of them will lodge in the lungs and cause death.

Initial treatment kills the adult worms, and subsequent treatments are designed to kill the microfilariae that remain in the bloodstream. This treatment process is lengthy, and it does involve a measure of risk. Some dogs who are successfully treated may continue to experience problems caused by organ damage and require ongoing maintenance to prevent congestive heart failure.

Provided no infection is already present, a variety of preventives can protect your dog from the devastating effects of heartworms. Dog owners are currently limited to heartworm preventatives that have to be dosed daily or monthly from spring to fall to cover the entire mosquito season. Whether these products are applied orally or topically, there is the problem of remembering to administer the medication on a regular basis. Check with your veterinarian to find out which options are currently available.

COMMON HEALTH CONCERNS

Every breed of dog is susceptible to health problems, and Toy and Miniature Poodles are no exception. In the process of establishing consistent characteristics in a purebred dog, a certain amount of inbreeding is necessary. While this helps to produce offspring who will reliably represent a breed, inbreeding also increases the risk of inheriting genetic defects.

It may be overwhelming to think your dog has the potential for so many genetic problems, but realistically, the incidence of defects depends entirely on breeding. Sound breeding practices involve introducing genes from Toy and Miniature Poodles who are not closely related and culling from a breeding program those dogs who carry defect-producing genes. Recent scientific advances in genetic testing are providing the knowledge and tools for breeders to further reduce the incidence of disease in dogs.

Some of the following diseases and conditions have been found to occur at a higher frequency in the Poodle than in other breeds. Others have become common concerns for all dog owners. Becoming familiar with these conditions is helpful in evaluating a breeding program, choosing a dog, or recognizing symptoms and obtaining prompt treatment.

Allergies

Allergies are actually an inheritable condition, but the frequency of diagnosis makes them a common health concern for many dog owners. Allergies affect a great number of breeds, including Toy and Miniature Poodles, and can sometimes cause much frustration for veterinarians and dog owners in isolating the allergen source. The most common types of canine allergies are contact, inhalant, bacterial, food, and flea allergies.

Some Toy and Miniature Poodles may suffer from food allergies.

Contact Allergies

Contact allergies are rare in dogs, but instances occur when a dog develops a reaction when he comes in contact with certain substances like the chemicals in disinfectants, pesticides, or other products. A localized reaction ensues, resulting in irritation of the skin or swelling. Dog beds containing cedar have been known to cause allergic reactions in some dogs. This type of allergy can be controlled by removing the offending substance from the dog's environment.

Inhalant Allergies

Inhalant allergies are the most common allergies seen in dogs. They are caused by sensitivity to pollen, mold spores, or dust mites. Unlike people, inhalant allergies in dogs do not cause respiratory symptoms, but rather are manifested through the skin.

The dog becomes itchy and begins to scratch and bite at his body and legs. He may also shake his head, rub his face, or lick his feet. These symptoms appear seasonally for pollen allergies.

Your veterinarian can prescribe anti-inflammatories, corticosteroids, or antihistamines to relieve your dog's discomfort. Medicated shampoos help soothe the skin, and supplements containing omega-3 and omega-6 fatty acids help restore damaged skin. Allergy testing is currently available to determine the cause of inhalant allergies, and steps can be taken to minimize the dog's exposure to the allergen.

Bacterial Allergies

Bacterial allergies are caused when the dog's immune system is not capable of handling the staph bacteria that normally exist in the environment. The bacteria then cause infections in the skin called *pyoderma*. Intense itching, patchy hair loss, and flaky skin are the result. Veterinarians often prescribe topical or oral medication to treat this condition, and medicated shampoos and fatty acid supplements can provide symptom relief and help improve the quality of the skin.

Food Allergies

Food allergies are also manifested through the skin, with scratching and excessive shedding being the most noticeable symptoms. Food allergies can also cause digestive upset and diarrhea. This is probably the most frustrating type of canine allergy. Due to the number of ingredients in commercial dog food, it can be very difficult to determine the source of the allergen.

The course of action most often taken is to change the dog's diet to a food he has never eaten. Since food allergies develop after a dog is exposed to an allergen source over a period of time, changing to a completely different type of food results in a cessation of symptoms. Unfortunately, it takes at least two months on a new diet before symptoms dissipate and the allergen source can be confirmed. It takes time and patience to find a suitable diet for the food-allergic dog.

A number of pet food manufacturers now produce dog foods with unusual ingredients, such as rabbit or duck, which provide new diet options for allergic dogs. Several hypoallergenic prescription diets also are available through veterinarians. But adhering to a prescribed diet also means that treats and any other consumable product must meet the new dietary requirements. Any deviation from a prescribed diet will thwart attempts to diagnose the allergen and determine an appropriate diet.

Flea Allergies

Flea allergies are caused by a dog's sensitivity to flea saliva. When a flea bites a dog, it injects its saliva into the skin. For some dogs, this causes an intense reaction resulting in itching and scratching that can subsequently damage the skin and lead to secondary bacterial infections. The most obvious way to treat flea allergies is to get rid of the fleas.

Blood Disorders

Blood serves as a mode of transportation to deliver oxygen and nutrients to all the living cells of the body. It also has a safety feature called *clotting* that helps prevent excessive blood loss and that aids in healing when its transportation routes (veins, arteries, and capillaries) have been damaged. Blood disorders affect the blood's ability to perform these functions properly.

Von Willebrand's Disease

Von Willebrand's disease is a blood clotting disorder that can cause excessive bleeding. Blood platelets, the building blocks for blood clotting, are made up of 12 factors that allow them to function properly. Von Willebrand's disease affects factor 8 in this make-up and prevents the platelets from sticking together to form clots.

Young Toy and Miniature Poodles may show no indications of this disorder, even after tail docking, but the symptoms may arise later during sterilization or other surgery. A simple screening test before surgery is often performed by veterinarians to measure clotting time. If clotting time exceeds four minutes, it may indicate the presence of von Willebrand's disease. A specific blood test can then confirm if this is the case.

Other signs of the disease include unexplained nosebleeds, bleeding from the gums or other mucous membranes, and bruising under the skin. Three different grades of von Willebrand's disease occur, with Type I being the mildest form and Type III being the most severe. Like many other congenital diseases, no cure is possible, but the condition can be managed.

When hemorrhaging occurs or is expected during surgery, a transfusion of complete plasma or a blood product called *cryoprecipitate* will be necessary to temporarily boost the concentration of von Willebrand's factor in the blood. Dog owners can take precautions to prevent accidents, and certain drugs that affect blood clotting should be avoided. These include aspirin, antihistamines, and ibuprofen. Dogs with Type I may show few if any symptoms, and they may live relatively normal lives without complications.

Cancer

Cancer is the abnormal growth of cells that can invade and disrupt the functions of healthy tissue and organs. It has become one of the leading causes of death in dogs, so it is a great concern for all dog owners. Skin tumors afflict the Toy and Miniature Poodle more commonly than other types, so these warrant particular attention from Poodle owners, who should always be observant for signs of the disease.

Skin Tumors

Small skin tumors may begin to develop in the middle-aged to older dog, and Toy and Miniature Poodles seem especially prone to them. In most cases, they are benign and nothing to be concerned about, but any tumor should be brought to the attention of your veterinarian during checkups. Seek immediate attention for tumors that grow rapidly, change colors, or develop sores that refuse to heal.

Care should be taken to

Any tumor should be brought to the attention of your veterinarian.

avoid irritating skin tumors while grooming. Tumors located in sensitive areas like the rectum, lips, eyelids, or ears can be removed if they are easily irritated and cause problems for the dog. In most cases, though, benign skin tumors are best left alone.

Ear Infections

Ear infections are always a concern for floppy-eared dogs like the Poodle. Unlike dogs with erect ears, the Poodle's ears do not always receive adequate ventilation to keep the ear canals dry. The abundance of hair growth on a Poodle's ears additionally restricts airflow and traps moisture inside the ear. This dark, moist environment creates the perfect conditions for bacteria to multiply.

The most obvious sign of an ear infection is an unmistakable odor from the ears. Dogs with ear infections shake their heads frequently or scratch at their ears. Redness, excessive discharge, and pain may also be evident. Your veterinarian can prescribe topical ointments or oral antibiotics, depending on the severity of the infection, but he will also want to determine the underlying cause of the infection.

For Toy and Miniature Poodles, many cases of ear infections are due to a lack of ear maintenance. It is very important to remove hair growth from the ear canals and clean the ears regularly. Isopropyl alcohol can be used as a cleaning and drying agent by applying it with a cotton ball or cotton-tipped swab. Putting cotton balls in your dog's ears prior to bathing also helps keep moisture out of the ears.

Other causes of ear infections include allergies, parasites, and thyroid dysfunction. Your veterinarian should investigate these possibilities if a more obvious cause cannot be found. In very serious cases, your veterinarian may want to thoroughly flush and clean the ears under sedation before treating with antibiotic medications.

Endocrine System Disorders

The endocrine system consists of hormones and the glands that secrete them. Some hormones influence growth and development, some regulate metabolism, and some are responsible for reproductive functions or other bodily processes. Because hormones affect so many different tissues and organs in the body, disorders of the endocrine system can result in a great variety of

Signs of an Ear Infection

The following are signs that your Poodle may be suffering from an ear infection:

- odor from the ears
- frequent head shaking or ear scratching
- redness, excessive discharge, or pain

symptoms. To complicate matters, hormone levels can be affected by other factors, such as stress or illness, so proper diagnosis is required to determine if an endocrine system disorder is responsible for a health condition.

Hypothyroidism/Lymphocytic Thyroiditis

Lymphocytic thyroiditis is caused when the body's autoimmune system attacks the thyroid gland. The thyroid gland is located in the dog's neck and is responsible for regulating metabolic rate by producing hormones. When the thyroid gland is damaged by the assault of white blood cells, it can no longer produce adequate amounts of hormones, a condition called *hypothyroidism*.

This type of thyroid disease is the most common inherited endocrine disorder in dogs, so it is not surprising that Toy and Miniature Poodles are also on the list of susceptible breeds. Because the endocrine system maintains a delicate balance of hormones within the body, symptoms of thyroid dysfunction are varied and sometimes misleading. Skin problems, hair loss, weight loss, weight gain, lethargy, intolerance to the cold, and behavioral changes are all symptoms linked to thyroid malfunction.

Tests to confirm hypothyroidism diagnoses likewise do not always produce definitive results. Blood tests used to measure thyroid hormones can be influenced by a number of factors, including heat cycles, medications, and general health. Sometimes it only takes a slight deviation from normal hormone levels to produce symptoms. Very often, when no other cause can be found for symptoms, diagnosis is confirmed when thyroid treatment shows positive results.

The good news is that this condition is very easily treated using hormone supplementation in the form of pills administered twice per day. The pills are small and easily concealed in a piece of cheese or hot dog included with the dog's meals. Treatment must be continued for the life of the dog, but it is relatively inexpensive, and the prognosis for a long, healthy life is very good.

Treating Hypothyroidism

Hypothyroidism is easily treated using hormone supplementation in the form of pills administered twice per day. Although treatment must be continued for the life of the dog, it is relatively inexpensive, and the prognosis is good.

Cushing's Disease

Also called *hyperadrenocorticism*, Cushing's disease is caused by an excess of cortisol in the body. It generally affects older dogs and produces a number of symptoms, such as hair loss, a distended abdomen, muscle weakness, and frequent urination, which are often dismissed as age-related maladies. Other symptoms of this disorder include increased appetite, high blood pressure, skin abnormalities, and urinary tract infections.

The disease is caused by a malfunction of the adrenal or pituitary gland, most often the result of a tumor. Blood tests can provide an accurate diagnosis. In the case of an adrenal gland tumor, the condition can be cured with the removal of the tumor. Unfortunately, about half of adrenal tumors are malignant, and there is the possibility that the malignancy will have already spread to other areas of the body. Pituitary gland tumors are usually treated using drug therapy, and management of the condition will require medications for the life of the dog.

If left untreated, Cushing's disease can contribute to other life-threatening conditions, such as congestive heart failure, liver and kidney failure, or diabetes, so it is important to seek prompt veterinary care. Most dogs who receive proper treatment have a greatly improved quality of life and can live well into their golden years.

Diabetes Mellitus

Diabetes mellitus is the result of an insufficient production of insulin by the pancreas. Without enough insulin, the dog's body cannot process sugars as a source of energy, which causes an increase in blood glucose levels. The pancreatic failure in each dog is different, with the production of insulin ranging from low levels to none at all. Cells in the body that are deprived of the life-sustaining energy they need begin to die, which can ultimately affect the function of organs, vision, and circulation.

Symptoms of diabetes mellitus include increased appetite and water consumption, frequent urination, lack of energy, and weight loss. Diagnosis is easily made by detecting glucose in the urine or high glucose levels in the blood. Dogs with a mild form of the disease may be treated with the use of a special diet and regular exercise. More serious cases require the administration of insulin injections.

This is an extremely high-maintenance condition that requires precision in feeding the dog a measured amount of food at the exact same times each day. Insulin injections, which are administered subcutaneously (under the skin), must also be provided on a very strict schedule. When blood glucose levels are kept under control, organ and tissue damage is minimized, and the dog can expect reasonable longevity and a good quality of life.

Eye Disorders

Toy and Miniature Poodles are particularly prone to eye problems, and this should be taken into consideration when choosing or breeding a Poodle. Because vision is such a vital sense, Poodle owners should be on the alert for any symptoms of eye disorders and seek immediate veterinary attention for any problems. Most eye conditions are considered emergencies, as they demand prompt treatment to prevent permanent damage to sight.

Cataracts

A cataract is any opacity within the eye lens that causes an obstruction of vision. It is a progressive condition that begins as a small spot on the lens and has little effect on vision. The spot gradually enlarges to fill the lens, and it eventually causes complete blindness. The rate of progression may be rapid or occur slowly over several years.

Although cataracts may be caused by an eye injury or diabetes, they are usually inherited. Cataracts tend to develop in older dogs but should not be confused with the normal hardening of the lens that aged canines experience. When the lens hardens with age, it becomes grayish in appearance and results in slightly reduced vision, but a mature cataract will fill the lens with an opaque white obstruction that destroys functional vision.

Seek immediate veterinary attention if your Poodle seems to be experiencing any vision problems.

No treatments are available to prevent or cure cataracts. The only option is to remove the diseased lens and replace it with an artificial lens. Although cataract surgery has a very high success rate, it does not come cheap. This type of surgery must be performed with specialized equipment by a veterinary ophthalmologist who has advanced training in eye surgery.

Without surgery, cataracts can cause inflammation within the eye, which can result in glaucoma or a detached retina. Once inflammation occurs, it becomes a complication for cataract surgery, so it is best to have surgery performed as early as possible in the progression of the disease.

Entropion

Entropion involves the inward rolling of the eyelid, which causes the eyelashes to continuously irritate the eye. This is one of the many inheritable eye conditions that have been known to plague Poodles. Inherited entropion usually becomes evident within the first few months of age and generally affects the lower eyelids of one or both eyes. Symptoms include tearing, squinting, discharge from the eyes, and eye rubbing.

A thorough ocular examination is necessary to diagnose entropion, and surgical intervention is the only option for treatment. Veterinarians often "tack" the eyelid on a young dog by suturing it into a nondamaging position until the dog is old enough for permanent eyelid surgery. If left untreated, entropion can result in corneal ulcers or scarring that can permanently affect vision.

Epiphora

Epiphora is actually a symptom rather than a specific condition. It refers to the abnormal overflow of tears onto the face, which can leave brown stains on the fur at the corner of the eyes. It can be caused by the overproduction of tears that overwhelm the normal drainage system of the eye, irritation of the eye, or an abnormality in the drainage duct that restricts or prevents the drainage of tears. Signs of epiphora indicate a need for veterinary counseling to determine the cause.

An excess production of tears from an overactive lacrimal (tear) gland is an uncommon cause of epiphora, but it does occur. Although it may not cause any problems for the eye, the moisture and tear residue can irritate the skin under the eye and cause bacterial infections. The hair at the corner of the eye should be kept

Genetic Research Offers Hope

It is estimated that one-quarter of all purebred dogs are affected by or carriers of inheritable diseases. Scientists in the United States and Europe have successfully isolated the genes responsible for a number of inheritable conditions and have developed tests to detect some of them. Research to map the canine genome continues at a feverish pace, accelerating with scientific advancements and aided by funding from groups such as the AKC Canine Health Foundation. Such progress offers hope that the incidence of genetic diseases in dogs will eventually decline with the application of new knowledge and testing to breeding practices.

trimmed short and the skin kept as clean as possible. Regular wiping with hydrogen peroxide helps to prevent infection and also helps to bleach out the stain.

Epiphora is most likely a symptom of irritation to the eye, which is indicated by squinting or rubbing at the eyes. Toy and Miniature Poodles are susceptible to an inheritable condition called *distichiasis*, in which extra eyelashes grow from the inside edge of the eyelid and rub against the cornea to cause irritation or corneal ulcers. Surgical options are available to correct this problem.

Lacrimal duct atresia is another inheritable condition in Toy and Miniature Poodles that can cause epiphora. In this case, the lacrimal duct, which is the drainage tube for the eye, does not open into the eye as it should. This condition can be surgically treated by making an incision to open the duct and facilitate proper drainage.

Glaucoma

Glaucoma is a common cause of blindness in dogs. It may be a secondary condition caused by a number of eye disorders, such as luxation of the lens, eye tumors, or injuries to the eye, but in most cases it is a hereditary condition caused by abnormal drainage of the eye fluid. When fluid inside the eye does not drain properly, it causes a build-up of pressure within the eye that can permanently damage the retina and optic nerve. Some cases of glaucoma progress rapidly, resulting in permanent loss of vision within 24 hours, while other cases involve a gradual increase in eye pressure over several weeks or months, with visual impairment progressing more slowly.

Two types of inheritable glaucoma affect Toy and Miniature Poodles. *Narrow-angle* glaucoma affects the junction where the base of the iris joins the bottom of the cornea, called the *iridocorneal angle*. This is where fluids from inside the eye normally drain. When the iris is too far forward at its base, it prevents adequate drainage of eye fluids and results in increased pressure within the eye. Poodles are also susceptible to *goniodysgenesis*, the second type of glaucoma, which is the abnormal growth of tissue within the iridocorneal angle. This condition also restricts the drainage of eye fluid.

In either case, increased eye pressure results in symptoms such as an enlarged eye, a red or inflamed eye, cloudiness in the eye, dilated pupil, squinting, loss of appetite, and blindness. Acute glaucoma is a very painful, serious condition that requires emergency treatment to relieve the eye pressure.

Medical treatment may consist of intravenous or oral medication, eye drops, or surgery. Therapy to manage the condition is usually required for the life of the dog. Many dogs respond well to treatment, but a risk is present that the problem will eventually affect both eyes. There is also a good chance that dogs with inheritable glaucoma will eventually lose their vision completely.

Progressive Retinal Atrophy

Progressive retinal atrophy (PRA) is a progressive, hereditary disease that damages the retina in the eye and eventually leads to blindness. Unlike other breeds that are susceptible to early onset of this disease, Toy and Miniature Poodles tend to develop PRA in adulthood.

Did You Know?

Unlike other breeds that are susceptible to early onset of progressive retinal atrophy, Toy and Miniature Poodles tend to develop PRA in adulthood.

The initial symptom is reduced vision in dim light, referred to as night blindness. As the condition progresses, daytime vision diminishes, the pupils in the eyes become dilated in an attempt to gather more light, and the lens of the eye may become cloudy or develop cataracts. No cure is available for this condition, and total blindness eventually results.

Gastrointestinal Disorders

The gastrointestinal tract—also referred to as the GI tract—is a system of organs that processes food. The GI tract processes food, extracts energy and nutrients from food, and then expels the waste that is left over. Like people, dogs can experience digestive upset occasionally, but knowing how to tell the difference between mild indigestion and severe gastrointestinal distress can save your dog's life.

Diarrhea

Diarrhea can be caused by something as simple as changing to a new dog food too abruptly, or it could be a sign of serious intestinal distress. When other symptoms, such as vomiting, pain, weakness, severe straining, or blood in the stool are present, you should consult your veterinarian. You should also seek professional help if diarrhea persists for an extended period or occurs frequently, because persistent bouts of diarrhea can cause dehydration.

If diarrhea is the only symptom, you can withhold food for 12 to 24 hours to give the bowels a rest. Continue to provide water during this time. Minor cases of diarrhea usually disappear within 24 hours. Monitor your dog and check the consistency of his stools after you resume his normal feeding schedule. Your veterinarian can recommend over-the-counter medications to manage mild cases of diarrhea.

Vomiting

Vomiting can also be caused by something as minor as an upset stomach, or it could be a sign of serious illness. If your dog otherwise seems active and alert, you can withhold food and water for a while to see if vomiting ceases. Two to four hours after vomiting has stopped, you can begin to offer small amounts of water and food.

It is not unusual for dogs to eat grass occasionally and then vomit their stomach contents. While no one knows exactly why dogs do this, it is not considered a condition warranting concern. Some dogs are prone to stomach upset, and aged dogs can also develop sensitive stomachs, both of which can be managed with dietary restrictions. If vomiting persists or your dog displays any other symptoms, you should see your veterinarian immediately.

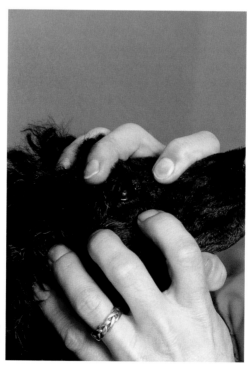

A comprehensive grooming routine can help expose some potentially serious diseases.

Neurological Disorders

The nervous system is responsible for delivering messages from the brain to various parts of the body. These messages control many functions, including breathing, muscle movement, and consciousness. When the messages produced by the brain are defective, or when messages are disrupted in their course through the nervous system, neurological dysfunction results. Involuntary muscle movement, incoordination, seizures, vision problems, and paralysis are all symptoms of neurological disorders.

Toy and Miniature Poodles occasionally suffer from neurological problems, and the exact causes and specific cures are elusive. But as research progresses in this area, treating and managing these conditions should become easier.

Causes of Seizures

Seizures in dogs can have a number of underlying physical causes, including hypoglycemia, thyroid dysfunction, lead poisoning, brain lesions, encephalitis, diabetes, and distemper.

Epilepsy

Witnessing a dog in seizure is a most frightening experience. The dog collapses, and muscles begin to contract involuntarily, sometimes wildly, with legs paddling, head jerking, and mouth snapping at the air. His body may become stiff or shake uncontrollably. He may drool or froth at the mouth. But when the seizure is over, the dog may appear quite calm and no worse for the wear.

Seizures in dogs can have a number of underlying physical causes; in fact, hypoglycemia, thyroid dysfunction, lead poisoning, brain lesions, encephalitis, diabetes, and distemper can all result in seizures. Blood and urine tests are necessary to determine if illness, injury, or a chemical imbalance is responsible. When these tests reveal no abnormalities, *idiopathic epilepsy* is suspected. This is an inheritable disorder that causes neurological dysfunction. An abnormal nerve-signal burst from the brain creates a chain-reaction of uncoordinated signals that result in a seizure. A mild seizure is called a *petit mal* seizure, and more serious seizures are referred to as *grand mal*. Unfortunately, the Poodle is one of the breeds known to inherit this frightening disorder.

Any seizure, of course, should receive veterinary attention, but seizures that are long in duration (over 3 minutes) or that occur frequently (several seizures within a 24-hour period) may be life threatening and should be considered emergencies. No cure exists, but epilepsy can be controlled through the use of medications that reduce the frequency of seizures. A change in diet can also provide some relief by eliminating the consumption of preservatives and chemical dyes that may trigger seizures. Occasionally, a dog who has been treated for epilepsy over a period of time can be slowly weaned off the medication and never experience further seizures.

Narcolepsy

Narcolepsy is a neurological disorder that causes a dog to collapse spontaneously into a deep sleep. These sleep attacks occur suddenly, often prior to an exciting event such as mealtime, playtime, or in anticipation of a human buddy's return. Narcolepsy is hereditary in 15 breeds of dog, including the Miniature Poodle.

The onset of symptoms usually begins at a young age, between four weeks and six months of age, and the attacks can occur as often as 100 times a day or as infrequently as once per year. Fortunately, little health risk is associated with narcolepsy, but dogs who suffer from it should be protected from dangerous situations that could lead to an injurious fall. Limiting the dog's access to stairs, window ledges, and similar high surfaces is advisable.

While no cure exists for the condition, it can be managed with medication to lessen the frequency of attacks. In some cases, a dog may outgrow narcolepsy. In other cases, the condition may worsen, even while on medication. If you suspect your dog suffers from this disorder, seek immediate veterinary attention.

The gene responsible for narcolepsy has been identified in certain breeds of dogs, and an accurate blood test is available to screen for carriers of this defect in Labrador Retrievers, Dobermans, and Dachshunds. A test for Poodles is currently in the developmental stages. As research progresses, these tests will become a valuable tool to help dog breeders eliminate the defective genes from their breeding lines.

Orthopedic Disorders

Orthopedic disorders affect the structure and function of a dog's skeletal system, including the bones, tendons, ligaments, muscles, and joints. Toy and Miniature Poodles are known to suffer from a few common orthopedic disorders that can cause significant discomfort for them. The good news is that, in many cases, these conditions are manageable or correctable.

Legg-Calve-Perthes Disease (LCP)

Legg-Calve-Perthes disease causes a loss of blood supply to the ball portion of the hip joint and eventually leads to deterioration of the bone and cartilage. Signs of the disease usually become evident between 4 and 11 months of age, when the dog displays pain and lameness in a rear leg. The condition can be confirmed with x-rays, and treatment depends on the severity of each case.

Many cases can be treated through the use of nonsurgical therapy, especially in the early stages, but surgical repair becomes necessary when arthritis and pain cannot be medically managed. Surgery involves excising a portion of the femoral head to help eliminate the painful bony contact in the hip joint. Recovery can be slow, but the quality of life for the dog can greatly improve. Some dogs may experience recurring lameness, especially after heavy exercise or weather changes, and the use of pain relief and anti-inflammatory drugs may be required for ongoing maintenance.

Medial Patellar Luxation

Medial patellar luxation is a congenital defect that causes the kneecap, or patella, to dislocate from its normal position. Medial luxation refers to the shifting of the kneecap to the inside of the leg, which is the most common form of patellar luxation in dogs. This condition is a concern for a number of small-breed dogs, including Toy and Miniature Poodles.

The defect involves the improper attachment of the patellar ligament. This ligament runs from the bottom of the kneecap to the tibia (shinbone), and when it is attached too far to the inside of the leg instead of the midline of the leg, it puts pressure on the kneecap that causes it to dislodge from its groove in the femur (thighbone). Each time muscles are contracted to bend the knee, the pressure on the kneecap causes wear against the groove until the kneecap begins to slide out of place easily.

Symptoms revolve around the discomfort associated with a dislocated kneecap. The dog may show constant or intermittent lameness, difficulty walking or jumping, or he may hold a leg out to the side when walking.

Some dogs can tolerate this condition for many years or possibly a lifetime. They may even learn how to snap the kneecap back into position on their own. Others may require surgical correction. The condition is graded according to severity, with Grades I and II being the mildest forms, and Grades III and IV being the most severe. Grades I and II may be completely asymptomatic, while Grades III and IV will require veterinary intervention.

Restraint Options

When dealing with a sick or injured animal, always take precautions to protect yourself from injury by restraining the dog when necessary. A few restraint and transportation techniques can be used to handle and transport a seriously ill or injured dog:

- **Muzzle**—Can be constructed from a strip of cloth or rope. Tie it around the muzzle with a single knot under the jaw and the ends drawn around under the ears to be tied at the base of the skull. Should not be used on dogs who have difficulty breathing or who are suffering from a serious mouth injury.

- **Body wrap**—Can be improvised using a blanket or large towel, wrapped around the dog with his legs carefully folded under him to keep him from struggling.

- **Stretcher**—A board, blanket, or floor mat can be used to support and carry the dog's body. The item should be supported at both ends, usually requiring the assistance of another person.

The surgery to repair this defect consists of deepening the groove in which the patella rides, and possibly relocating the patellar ligament. The condition can affect one leg more than the other, but in some cases, both legs will need surgical attention. With or without surgery, most dogs with medial patellar luxation experience some degree of arthritis as they age.

EMERGENCIES AND FIRST AID

Emergencies can happen anywhere, at any time. In some situations, you must provide medical attention for your dog when a veterinarian is not immediately available. First-aid procedures can save your dog's life and increase the chance of a healthy recovery.

Checking Vital Signs

Checking the vital signs of your dog greatly assists a veterinarian in the initial evaluation of your dog's condition. This information can be especially helpful if you need to seek professional advice by phone before transporting your dog to a medical facility.

- **The normal temperature range for dogs is 100° to 102.5°F (37.8° to 39.2°C).** To check your dog's temperature, you need a rectal thermometer made for animal use. The tip of the thermometer can be lubricated with petroleum jelly and then inserted about 1 inch (2.5 cm) into the rectum while holding the dog's tail up. It should slide in easily. Do not force the insertion, or you could possibly puncture the bowel. Digital thermometers are safer than glass thermometers and will alert you when an accurate temperature has been recorded. Your veterinarian may be willing to instruct you in this procedure during routine exams, and it is a good idea to practice this skill prior to an emergency. Taking your dog's temperature when he is healthy allows you to make note of his normal temperature so that you can detect even slight elevations. If you are not comfortable performing this particular vital sign check, noting other vital signs will still provide important information for your veterinarian.

- **The normal pulse rate for small dogs is 90 to 120 beats per minute (bpm).** The easiest place to check the pulse is on the inside of the hind leg where the femoral artery is located. Place your hand on the inside of the leg near the groin, and move your fingers back and forth until you can feel the pulse. Count the number of pulses in 15 seconds and multiply it by four to get the beats per minute. You should practice locating this artery when your dog is healthy so that you can find it easily in an emergency.

- **The normal respiration rate for dogs is 10 to 30 breaths per minute.** Respiration rates for Toy and Miniature Poodles are on the higher end of that range due to their smaller size and excitable nature. Count your dog's chest expansions for 15 seconds and multiply it by four to determine the breaths per minute. Take note if your dog's breathing is weak, shallow, or labored. These are important diagnostic signs that will assist your veterinarian.

Cardiopulmonary Resuscitation (CPR)

Cardiopulmonary resuscitation (CPR) is used when an animal has stopped breathing and the heart has stopped beating. There are occasions when breathing has stopped but a pulse can still be detected, in which case rescue breathing can be attempted without performing heart massage.

To perform rescue breathing, first make sure that the dog does not have an obstructed airway by checking inside the mouth and throat. Then, with the dog lying on his side, extend his neck so that the throat is straight, and hold his mouth shut with your hand. Gently blow into his nose until his chest expands. For Toy

Your veterinarian can show you how to take your Poodle's temperature properly.

- bandage scissors
- Benadryl
- buffered aspirin
- cotton swabs
- dosage chart
- emergency information
- epsom salts
- eye wash
- first-aid tape
- gauze rolls
- hydrogen peroxide
- muzzle
- oral syringe
- pet first-aid guide
- petroleum jelly
- rectal thermometer
- rubbing alcohol
- sterile gauze pads (different sizes)
- triple antibiotic ointment
- tweezers
- vet wrap bandages

and Miniature Poodles, small puffs of breath should be sufficient to fill the lungs. Repeat this procedure several times. If air does not go into the dog, a hidden obstruction may be present, and you will have to treat him for choking (see common emergencies) before performing CPR.

To apply heart massage, place your flat hand on the lower half of the dog's chest just behind the elbow, and compress the chest about 1 inch (2.5 cm) with a thrusting push. Remember, Toy and Miniature Poodles are small dogs, and you do not need to apply great force. Repeat this procedure five times, and check to see if pulse or breathing has resumed. If not, continue a cycle of five rescue breaths, five heart massages, and a vital sign check until breathing and heart rate have resumed. When breathing and heart rate have been restored, you should seek veterinary attention immediately.

Common Emergencies

Good breeding and health maintenance practices may help prevent disease and illness, but they do nothing to protect your dog from accidents. Common sense and safety precautions are the best accident preventives, and yet the chance always exists that a health-related situation may arise through no fault of your own. Being prepared for these situations can mean avoiding more serious physical damage or saving the life of your dog.

Bleeding

Severe external bleeding requires your assistance to prevent too much loss of blood. Use a heavy gauze pad or clean cloth to press against the wound to minimize the flow of blood. Only use a tourniquet as a last resort in the case of life-threatening blood loss from a limb. The tourniquet should be applied between the wound and the heart, and it should be loosened for 20 seconds every 15 minutes. Although tourniquets do stop the bleeding, they also stop circulation of blood to the limb, which can cause permanent damage and result in amputation. Serious bleeding requires prompt veterinary treatment.

Signs of internal bleeding include bleeding from the nose, mouth, or rectum. Other signs of internal bleeding include coughing blood, blood in the urine, pale gums, and abdominal distension or pain. If your dog shows signs of internal bleeding, wrap him in a blanket to keep him as warm as possible, and seek veterinary attention immediately.

Fractures

Fractures are extremely painful, and caution should be used in handling the dog. Use a muzzle to ensure your safety, and try to control any bleeding. Then, transport the dog to the veterinarian on a stretcher. Do not attempt to set the fracture yourself. If you need to stabilize the limb, you can wrap the leg in cotton padding and tape a rolled-up newspaper around it. The splint should be long enough to extend beyond the joints above and below the fracture.

Shock

Serious injury or extreme fright can cause a dog to go into shock, a potentially fatal condition. Shock is the body's response to trauma or loss of blood. It causes blood pressure to drop to a dangerous level. Low blood pressure, in turn, causes a lack of blood supply that can damage cells and reduce the function of body systems. Signs of shock include shallow or irregular breathing, dilated pupils, weak pulse, and a dazed appearance.

Keep the dog as quiet and calm as possible, restraining him if necessary. Provide a blanket for warmth, and keep his head level with the rest of his body. Then, seek veterinary attention immediately.

Burns

Burns are an extremely painful injury that may require the use of a muzzle for your safety. If your dog experiences a burn due to contact with a chemical, flush the area immediately with large quantities of cold water, apply cold compresses, and seek the attention of a veterinarian.

Burns resulting from exposure to a heat source should be flushed

Medical emergencies require immediate veterinary care.

Common Dog-Related Emergencies

The following are common dog-related emergencies:

- bleeding
- fractures
- shock
- burns
- choking
- cuts and abrasions
- heatstroke
- frostbite and hypothermia
- poisoning
- snakebites
- insect bites and stings
- seizures

immediately with cool water. The sooner you can cool the burned area, the less damage will be done to the tissues. It may take some time for tissues to react to a burn, so do not wait for symptoms of blistering, swelling, and red skin to appear before initiating treatment. Large burn areas can be cooled by wrapping the dog in a towel soaked with cool water. After cooling the burn, apply a cold compress until you can get to the veterinarian.

Choking

When a dog chokes, he may attempt to cough up the object or begin to gag or paw at his mouth. If a foreign object is visible in his throat, you can attempt to remove the object with your fingers, pliers, or tweezers. Be careful not to push the object farther into the throat. You may need the assistance of another person to hold the dog, and care should be used to prevent a bite.

If the object is not visible or the dog is too panicked to manually remove the object, place your hands on each side of the dog's chest and compress the chest in a quick thrusting motion. You may need to repeat this procedure a few times until the air from the lungs forces the object out. Minor choking cases may not require veterinary attention, but you should have your dog checked out if you suspect any damage to the throat. Even after an object is removed, throat swelling can severely restrict airflow to the lungs.

Cuts and Abrasions

Minor cuts and abrasions can be treated at home. Flush the area thoroughly with water, and be meticulous about removing all dirt and debris. Apply an antibiotic cream twice a day until the injury has healed. For minor injuries that won't seem to heal, or for more serious cuts and abrasions larger than 1 inch (2.5 cm) long, seek veterinary attention.

Heatstroke

Heatstroke can be fatal if not treated immediately. A dog suffering from heatstroke has an extremely high body temperature and may vomit, collapse, or have difficulty breathing. You must cool his body as rapidly as possible by placing him in a tub of cool water, wrapping him in a cold, wet towel, or soaking him with a garden hose. Be sure to cool the areas on his underside and inside the legs. Seek immediate veterinary attention for this dangerous condition.

Frostbite and Hypothermia

Toy and Miniature Poodles do not have the body mass or blood volume that larger dogs have, which makes them more prone to suffering frostbite or hypothermia in colder climates. You may notice your small Poodle stepping gingerly or skipping with his rear legs to avoid touching frozen ground. You can avoid problems by limiting your dog's outdoor time during extremely frigid weather, letting his coat grow a little longer in the winter, restricting him from deep snow that tends to adhere to his fur, or dressing him in a dog coat or boots to protect him from the cold.

Signs that your dog has been overexposed to the cold include shivering, limping, accumulation of ice on the body and limbs, redness or discoloration of the skin, and weakness. In the case of hypothermia, your dog's body temperature will be below normal.

If you suspect your dog has frostbite, you can warm the affected area with a towel soaked in lukewarm water. Dry the area gently after it has been warmed. You should not attempt to rub or massage the area, because this can damage frozen tissues.

Hypothermia can be treated by using a blanket and a hot water bottle or hot pack to warm your dog. Do not place a hot water bottle or hot pack directly on your dog, because these can be too hot and cause burns. It is best to wrap them in a towel first to provide a gentle, radiant heat. When your dog's temperature has returned to normal, stop warming him so that he does not become overheated.

Seek veterinary care if frostbite has left tissues discolored or numb, or in the case of hypothermia, because these are both very serious conditions.

Poisoning

If you suspect your dog has consumed a poisonous substance, do not attempt to induce vomiting without first consulting a veterinarian or calling the ASPCA Animal Poison Control Center Hotline at (888) 426-4435 (888-4ANI-HELP). Poisonings can result from the consumption of commercial products, medications, toxic plants, or dangerous foods. Signs of poisoning include vomiting, diarrhea, weakness, salivation, and convulsions. If you know what your dog consumed, write down the product information or take the item with you to the veterinarian.

It is always a good idea to have some hydrogen peroxide or syrup of ipecac on hand to induce vomiting when instructed to do so. Veterinary attention will be necessary in any case of poisoning.

You can help prevent poisonings by keeping all medications and dangerous substances out of reach of your dog.

Snakebites

The bite from a poisonous snake obviously requires immediate veterinary treatment, but you can help minimize tissue damage by flushing the bite area thoroughly with cool water. Also, keep the dog calm, because exercise speeds the spread of venom through the body. For those who plan to camp or travel in areas known to be snake territory, it is a good idea to make note of veterinary facilities in the vicinity so that you can seek prompt veterinary attention for such an emergency.

If you suspect that your Poodle has ingested something poisonous, get help right away.

Insect Bites and Stings

Most insect bites and stings are minor injuries that do not require treatment. But like people, some dogs are more sensitive to such things and will suffer a reaction to them. The possibility also exists that a dog will stumble into a bee's nest and become severely stung and show symptoms that include swelling around the stings, swelling of limbs, and pain.

Cortisone or anti-inflammatory ointment can be applied topically to bites or stings to provide some relief. For severe reactions, an over-the-counter antihistamine can be given orally, but you should contact your veterinarian for the correct dose.

Seizures

Seizures result in a loss of consciousness and a lack of muscle control that can cause a dog to thrash or snap violently. For your safety, you should never attempt to restrain a dog during a seizure, but you can help keep him safe by moving him away from stairs, breakable items, or furniture. You can further protect him from injury by placing blankets, pillows, or cushions around him until the seizure has subsided. Provide a quiet environment until the seizure abates, and keep the dog calm and quiet afterward. Any seizure is cause for immediate veterinary attention.

HOLISTIC HEALTH CARE

Holistic health care for animals is part of a trend toward more natural treatments for canine health conditions. Many veterinarians are receiving additional, specialized training in holistic medicine, which provides more options in canine health care. The use of natural healing techniques involving herbs, homeopathy, acupuncture, and chiropractic is helping to improve the lives of dogs and their owners.

Holistic treatment methods can be used to complement conventional medical treatments, or they can be applied as stand-alone treatments, depending on the health condition being treated. Certain situations in particular may indicate a need to investigate holistic alternatives. For example, if a dog has undesirable reactions to synthetic medications, or conventional treatments have proven ineffective, you may decide to try a holistic alternative. In some cases, holistic remedies can provide better benefits than are available through conventional methods.

When researching holistic health care alternatives, it is important to choose a board-certified veterinarian who has received training in the specific holistic field. The American Holistic Veterinary Medical Association (AHVMA) is comprised of members who practice various forms of complementary and alternative medicine. The organization provides a membership directory, organized by state, on its website at www.ahvma.org. Other organizations that offer training in specific areas of holistic health care can provide referrals for veterinarians certified through their organizations.

Herbs

Herbs have been used for centuries as remedies for a wide range of human ills and discomforts. The application of herbs to animal health is not as well documented, even though it has probably been used just as long. Herbs have been successfully used to treat a great variety of health conditions in dogs, including hot spots, allergies, arthritis, diabetes, liver disease, urinary tract infections, and upper respiratory infections. Depending on the form of the herb used and the condition being treated, herbal remedies may be applied orally or topically.

Some herbs function as dietary supplements, while others have the same properties and effects as drugs. For this reason, you should never assume that herbs are safe just because they are natural. Some herbs that are safe for humans are potentially dangerous for pets. Other herbs are known to interact with certain drugs or cause complications for dogs with certain health conditions.

Care must be taken in the prescription and use of herbs, and they should only be used under the direction of a veterinary herbalist. The Veterinary Botanical Medicine Association (VBMV) offers training and certification for veterinarians interested in the application of herbal medicine, and the association provides a directory of its members on its website at www.vbma.org for pet owners seeking referrals.

Homeopathy

Homeopathy is based on the principle that a medicine that causes similar symptoms as a disease can help cure that disease. Like other holistic treatments, homeopathy has ancient roots and seems to defy scientific validation. But while science cannot prove its effectiveness, it also cannot disprove it.

Homeopathic treatments involve taking a minute amount of substance that in larger doses would cause similar symptoms as the disease and administering the highly diluted substance to the

Disaster Preparedness

Natural disasters and the threat of terrorist attacks have put disaster preparedness at the forefront of people's minds. This preparedness should not exclude the canine member of your family. Who can forget the laments of those who have been forced to leave their animal companions behind in the rush to evacuate a dangerous situation? Being prepared for such situations will help you avoid the heartbreak of leaving your dog to fend for himself in the wake of a disaster.

Many people have taken the advice of authorities and prepared a disaster kit for the family or household members. A disaster kit can also be assembled for your dog. In addition, you should keep a list of animal shelters, kennels, and other places in your area that may assist with temporary lodging for your dog in an emergency.

The following items are necessities for your disaster kit:

- baby wipes (unscented)
- bottled water
- brushes/combs
- canned and dry food for approx. one week
- emergency information (photos, pet ID, immunization records, veterinary contact)
- leash
- medications
- pet carrier
- pet feeding dishes
- pet first-aid kit
- pet waste bags
- small blanket

patient. It is very possible that such treatment triggers an immune response that boosts a dog's defense against the disease.

The Academy of Veterinary Homeopathy (AVH) educates and certifies veterinarians in this holistic specialty and provides membership information on its website at www.theavh.org. Like other forms of holistic health care, dog owners should educate themselves on this form of treatment before seeking professional advice.

Acupuncture

Acupuncture is an ancient Chinese treatment that has established itself in the Western world as a viable treatment alternative for both humans and animals. Based on the Chinese principle of *chi*, which is the energy force that circulates through all living beings, channels are present along the skin through which life energy travels. When an imbalance or interruption in the flow of energy occurs, health is negatively affected.

The energy channels, called *meridians*, correspond to various organs and tissues throughout the body. Manipulating the energy force through these meridians influences healing by reestablishing the balance of energy in affected parts of the body. The meridians are stimulated by inserting tiny needles into the skin at specific acupuncture points. Modern acupuncturists sometimes use laser beams for this purpose.

Acupuncture is most often used by Western practitioners in the treatment of musculo-skeletal problems, but it has also been successfully used to treat reproductive, hormonal, neurological, psychological, and dermatological problems. Although science has not been able to determine exactly how acupuncture works, its proof of effectiveness lies in the many patients who have benefited from its application.

Another holistic treatment called *acupressure* is derived from the same principles that apply to acupuncture. Instead of using needles, acupuncture points are stimulated by applying pressure with fingers, hands, or elbows. This may seem like a more desirable alternative for those who are squeamish about needles, but veterinarians rarely offer this treatment. Instead, training is often offered directly to dog owners who wish to treat their own

Benefits of Chiropractic Care

Chiropractic care can benefit dogs who are suffering from musculoskeletal problems involving the neck, back, legs, or tail. It has also been noted as a remedy for internal disorders and is used as a supplement to conventional medicine to help speed recovery.

pets. Perhaps this is because it is considered safe and does not require as much expertise as acupuncture. For both acupuncture and acupressure, treatments must be repeated at regular intervals to achieve the maximum benefits.

The International Veterinary Acupuncture Society (IVAS) certifies veterinary acupuncturists and provides a directory of its members on its website at www.ivas.org. A national organization that represents veterinary acupuncturists is the American Academy of Veterinary Acupuncture (AAVA). Its website at www.aava.org provides valuable information about this specialty and also features a directory of members. Those seeking a qualified veterinary acupuncturist for their dog's health needs should investigate both organizations.

Chiropractic

Chiropractic care for humans continues to amass a large following, and similar care for animals is also growing in popularity. This treatment method applies physical adjustments to the head, neck, and spine, which in turn can affect healing in other parts of the body. Its benefits are mainly sought for dogs with musculoskeletal problems involving the neck, back, legs, or tail. It has also been noted as a remedy for internal disorders and as a supplement to conventional medicine to help speed recovery.

Chiropractic care does not need to be administered only during the presence of illness or injury, however. Regular care is often provided as part of a health-maintenance routine. Chiropractic exams include an evaluation of the dog's history, current health, and prior x-rays and medical tests. Chiropractors conduct a neurological exam and analyze stance, gait, and motion to determine what kind of adjustments may be necessary. The American Veterinary Chiropractic Association (AVCA) certifies veterinarians who specialize in this field, and a directory of certified veterinary chiropractors is available at www.animalchiropractic.org.

THE AGING TOY AND MINIATURE POODLE

The improvement in canine diets and the advancement of veterinary medicine has increased the longevity of dogs. Thus, more dog owners are faced with managing the needs of aging dogs, and they have to deal with a variety of problems that affect an older dog's quality of life. Many of these problems can be prevented, treated, or managed to keep an older dog healthy and comfortable during his golden years.

Obesity

Obesity is one of the most common problems for older dogs, but it is preventable with proper care and management. Diet changes must be considered for older dogs who show weight gain or a decrease in activity level.

Dental Disease

Dental disease is another common problem in senior dogs, which is why older dogs should have their teeth examined regularly by a veterinarian. Your veterinarian may recommend professional teeth cleanings, which are performed under general anesthesia, to maintain good oral health. Dentures are not available for the unfortunate canine senior who has lost his teeth!

Dogs should have their teeth examined regularly by a veterinarian.

Vision and Hearing Problems

Vision and hearing can decline with age, and you may notice your dog becoming less responsive to verbal commands or having difficulty seeing where you threw his ball. The lens of the eye hardens and becomes less flexible with age, which causes difficulty focusing. Provided cataracts are not present, this is part of the normal aging process, and treatment is not usually necessary. Most dogs preserve sufficient vision to retain a good quality of life.

Hearing loss is also an inevitable part of aging, provided it is not caused by an underlying health condition. You should check your older dog's ears frequently to make sure they are clean and healthy. You may have to speak louder so that your dog can hear you, and it helps to accompany your verbal commands with hand signals so that your dog doesn't have to rely entirely on his hearing. Age-related hearing loss occurs gradually, and many dogs adjust to this deficiency quite well.

Arthritis

Arthritis is a degenerative joint disease that creeps up gradually with age and can cause significant discomfort for the older dog. Your dog may have difficulty lying down, getting up, or climbing stairs. You may notice your dog having trouble jumping up on furniture, or he may display a slight limp during walks. Diet supplements can often help to keep joints supple, and your veterinarian can prescribe a number of anti-inflammatory medications to relieve discomfort. Aspirin is often used to provide occasional relief, but you should ask your veterinarian about the correct dosage and how frequently it can be used.

Regular, moderate exercise is probably the best way to keep joints in good condition and prevent stiffness. You can also help keep your dog comfortable by making sure his bed is not located in a cold, wet, or drafty area that can aggravate his condition. Pet supply manufacturers have not ignored the aging dog population, and they now produce a number of products designed to help the arthritic dog. Orthopedic dog beds, stairs and ramps for access to furniture or cars, and heated blankets are just some of the items available through pet stores and catalogs.

Urinary Problems

Urinary problems, including incontinence and frequent urination, are conditions that plague older dogs and cause frustration for dog owners. Reduced liver and kidney function often results in an excess consumption of water, and therefore, an increase in the frequency of elimination. To prevent accidents, be prepared to take your dog out more frequently as he gets older. Any increase in urination should be checked by your veterinarian to rule out diabetes or other causes.

Sometimes, the sphincter muscle that releases urine from the bladder becomes lax in old age and results in the dribbling of urine. This occurs because the production of hormones necessary to keep the sphincter in good muscle tone decreases in old age. A full bladder contributes to this type of incontinence, so taking your dog out more frequently may help. In addition, you may want to provide a washable dog bed that can be cleaned when necessary. Seek the advice of your veterinarian, because hormone therapy is sometimes an effective treatment for this problem.

Heart Disease

Heart disease is most often caused by a thickening or abnormality of the heart valves in the older dog. The abnormal flow of blood between the chambers of the heart eventually leads to heart enlargement and subsequent heart failure. Although no cure for this condition exists, its progression can be slowed with proper medical treatment. The earlier this condition is diagnosed, the better the chance of extending the dog's life.

Cancer

Cancer is a word that strikes fear in the hearts of those who face this diagnosis. But medical advances have changed the outcome of cancer diagnoses so that it no longer means a definitive death sentence. Many treatments available to people are now available for dogs as well, including chemotherapy, radiation therapy, and surgery. The actual prognosis depends on the type, location, and extent of the cancer. Early diagnosis is often critical, so remaining observant for any symptoms in an older dog can mean the difference between a cure and euthanasia.

The health of your dog depends on many factors, most of which are within your control. Preventative care, observation, early detection, prompt treatments, and emergency preparedness all hinge on your dedication to preserving your dog's good health. When you look at your healthy Toy or Miniature Poodle's bright eyes and find yourself smiling back at his happy doggy grin, you will realize it's all worth it. Because when your Poodle loves life, you do, too!

Disorders Affecting the Senior Dog

The following are disorders that commonly affect the aging Toy and Miniature Poodle:

obesity

dental disease

vision and hearing problems

arthritis

urinary problems

heart disease

cancer

THE AMERICAN KENNEL CLUB BREED STANDARD

The Standard for the Poodle (Toy variety) is the same as for the Standard and Minature varieties except as regards heights.

General Appearance, Carriage, and Condition: That of a very active, intelligent and elegant-appearing dog, squarely built, well proportioned, moving soundly and carrying himself proudly. Properly clipped in the traditional fashion and carefully groomed, the Poodle has about him an air of distinction and dignity peculiar to himself.

Size, Proportion, Substance: Size-The Standard Poodle is over 15 inches at the highest point of the shoulders. Any Poodle which is 15 inches or less in height shall be disqualified from competition as a Standard Poodle. **The Miniature Poodle** is 15 inches or under at the highest point of the shoulders, with a minimum height in excess of 10 inches. Any Poodle which is over 15 inches or is 10 inches or less at the highest point of the shoulders shall be disqualified from competition as a Miniature Poodle. **The Toy Poodle** is 10 inches or under at the highest point of the shoulders. Any Poodle which is more than 10 inches at the highest point of the shoulders shall be disqualified from competition as a Toy Poodle.

As long as the Toy Poodle is definitely a Toy Poodle, and the Miniature Poodle a Miniature Poodle, both in balance and proportion for the Variety, diminutiveness shall be the deciding factor when all other points are equal.

Proportion - To insure the desirable squarely built appearance, the length of body measured from the breastbone to the point of the rump approximates the height from the highest point of the shoulders to the ground.

Substance - Bone and muscle of both forelegs and hindlegs are in proportion to size of dog.

Head and Expression: *(a) Eyes*— very dark, oval in shape and set far enough apart and positioned to create an alert intelligent expression. *Major fault: eyes round, protruding, large or very light. (b) Ears*— hanging close to the head, set at or slightly below eye level. The ear leather is long, wide and thickly feathered; however, the ear fringe should not be of excessive length. *(c) Skull*— moderately rounded, with a slight but definite stop. Cheekbones and muscles flat. Length from occiput to stop about the same as length of muzzle. *(d) Muzzle*— long, straight and fine, with slight chiseling under the eyes. Strong without lippiness. The chin definite enough to preclude snipiness. *Major fault: lack of chin.* **Teeth**— white, strong and with a scissors bite. *Major fault: undershot, overshot, wry mouth.*

Neck, Topline, Body: *Neck* well proportioned, strong and long enough to permit the head to be carried high and with dignity. Skin snug at throat. The neck rises from strong, smoothly muscled shoulders. Major fault: ewe neck. The *topline* is level, neither sloping nor roached, from the highest point of the shoulder blade to the base of the tail, with the exception of a slight hollow just behind the shoulder.

Body (a) Chest deep and moderately wide with well sprung ribs. (b) The loin is short, broad and muscular. (c) Tail straight, set on high and carried up, docked of sufficient length to insure a balanced outline. Major fault: set low, curled, or carried over the back.

Forequarters: Strong, smoothly muscled shoulders. The shoulder blade is well laid back and approximately the same length as the upper foreleg. Major fault: steep shoulder.

(a) Forelegs - Straight and parallel when viewed from the front. When viewed from the side the elbow is directly below the highest point of the shoulder. The pasterns are strong. Dewclaws may be removed. Feet - The feet are rather small, oval in shape with toes well arched and cushioned on thick firm pads. Nails short but not excessively shortened. The feet turn neither in nor out. Major fault: paper or splay foot.

Hindquarters: The angulation of the hindquarters balances that of the forequarters. (a) Hind legs straight and parallel when viewed from the rear. Muscular with width in the region of the stifles which are well bent; femur and tibia are about equal in length; hock to heel short and perpendicular to the ground. When standing, the rear toes are only slightly behind the point of the rump. Major fault: cow-hocks.

Coat: *(a) Quality*—(1) Curly: of naturally harsh texture, dense throughout. (2) Corded: hanging in tight even cords of varying length; longer on mane or body coat, head, and ears; shorter on puffs, bracelets, and pompons. *(b) Clip*— A Poodle under 12 months may be shown in the "Puppy" clip. In all regular classes, Poodles 12 months or over must be shown in the "English Saddle" or "Continental" clip. In the Stud Dog and Brood Bitch classes and in a non-competitive Parade of Champions, Poodles may be shown in the "Sporting" clip. A Poodle shown in any other type of clip shall be disqualified.

(1) "Puppy"—A Poodle under a year old may be shown in the "Puppy" clip with the coat long. The face, throat, feet and base of the tail are shaved. The entire shaven foot is visible. There is a pompon on the end of the tail. In order to give a neat appearance and a smooth unbroken line, shaping of the coat is permissible. (2) "English Saddle"—In the "English Saddle" clip the face, throat, feet, forelegs and base of the tail are shaved, leaving puffs on the forelegs and a pompon on the end of the tail. The hindquarters are covered with a short blanket of hair except for a curved shaved area on each flank and two shaved bands on each hindleg. The entire shaven foot and a portion of the shaven leg above the puff are visible. The rest of the body is left in full coat but may be shaped in order to insure overall balance. (3) "Continental"—In the "Continental" clip, the face, throat, feet, and base of the tail are shaved. The hindquarters are shaved with pompons (optional) on the hips. The legs are shaved, leaving bracelets on the hindlegs and puffs on the forelegs. There is a pompon on the end of the tail. The entire shaven foot and a portion of the shaven foreleg above the puff are visible. The rest of the body is left in full coat but may be shaped in order to insure overall balance. (4) "Sporting"—In the "Sporting" clip, a Poodle shall be shown with face, feet, throat, and base of tail shaved, leaving a scissored cap on the top of the head and a pompon on the end of the tail. The rest of the body, and legs are clipped or scissored to follow the outline of the dog leaving a short blanket of coat no longer than one inch in length. The hair on the legs may be slightly longer than that on the body.
In all clips the hair of the topknot may be left free or held in place by elastic bands. The hair is only of sufficient length to present a smooth outline. "Topknot" refers only to hair on the skull, from stop to occiput. This is the only area where elastic bands may be used.

Color: The coat is an even and solid color at the skin. In blues, grays, silvers, browns, cafe-au-laits, apricots and creams the coat may show varying shades of the same color. This is frequently present in the somewhat darker feathering of the ears and in the tipping of the ruff. While clear colors are definitely preferred, such natural variation in the shading of the coat is not to be considered a fault. Brown and cafe-au-lait Poodles have liver-colored noses, eye-rims and lips, dark toenails and dark amber eyes. Black, blue, gray, silver, cream and white Poodles have black noses, eye-rims and lips, black or self colored toenails and very dark eyes. In the apricots while the foregoing coloring is preferred, liver-colored noses, eye-rims and lips, and amber eyes are permitted but are not desirable. Major fault: color of nose, lips and eye-rims incomplete, or of wrong color for color of dog. Parti-colored dogs shall be disqualified. The coat of a parti-colored dog is not an even solid color at the skin but is of two or more colors.

Gait: A straightforward trot with light springy action and strong hindquarters drive. Head and tail carried up. Sound effortless movement is essential.

Temperament: Carrying himself proudly, very active, intelligent, the Poodle has about him an air of distinction and dignity peculiar to himself. Major fault: shyness or sharpness.

Major Faults: Any distinct deviation from the desired characteristics described in the Breed Standard.

Disqualifications: Size— A dog over or under the height limits specified shall be disqualified. Clip— A dog in any type of clip other than those listed under coat shall be disqualified. Parti-colors— The coat of a parti-colored dog is not an even solid color at the skin but of two or more colors. Parti-colored dogs shall be disqualified.

Value of Points
General appearance, temperament, carriage and condition.......30
Head, expression, ears, eyes and teeth.......20
Body, neck, legs, feet and tail.......20
Gait.......20
Coat, color and texture.......10

Approved August 14, 1984
Reformatted March 27, 1990

ASSOCIATIONS AND ORGANIZATIONS

BREED CLUBS

American Kennel Club (AKC)
5580 Centerview Drive
Raleigh, NC 27606
Telephone: (919) 233-9767
Fax: (919) 233-3627
E-mail: info@akc.org
www.akc.org

Canadian Kennel Club (CKC)
89 Skyway Avenue, Suite 100
Etobicoke, Ontario M9W 6R4
Telephone: (416) 675-5511
Fax: (416) 675-6506
E-mail: information@ckc.ca
www.ckc.ca

The Kennel Club
1 Clarges Street
London
W1J 8AB
Telephone: 0870 606 6750
Fax: 0207 518 1058
www.the-kennel-club.org.uk

The Poodle Club of America
Corresponding Secretary: Helen Tomb-Taylor
E-mail (general inquiries):
pca@poodleclubofamerica.org
www.poodleclubofamerica.org

United Kennel Club (UKC)
100 E. Kilgore Road
Kalamazoo, MI 49002-5584
Telephone: (269) 343-9020
Fax: (269) 343-7037
E-mail: pbickell@ukcdogs.com
www.ukcdogs.com

RESCUE ORGANIZATIONS AND ANIMAL WELFARE GROUPS

American Humane Association (AHA)
63 Inverness Drive East
Englewood, CO 80112
Telephone: (303) 792-9900
Fax: 792-5333
www.americanhumane.org

American Society for the Prevention of Cruelty to Animals (ASPCA)
424 E. 92nd Street
New York, NY 10128-6804
Telephone: (212) 876-7700
www.aspca.org

Royal Society for the Prevention of Cruelty to Animals (RSPCA)
Telephone: 0870 3335 999
Fax: 0870 7530 284
www.rspca.org.uk

The Humane Society of the United States (HSUS)
2100 L Street, NW
Washington DC 20037
Telephone: (202) 452-1100
www.hsus.org

SPORTS

Canine Freestyle Federation, Inc.
Membership Secretary: Brandy Clymire
E-mail: CFFmemberinfo@aol.com
www.canine-freestyle.org

International Agility Link (IAL)
Global Administrator: Steve Drinkwater
E-mail: yunde@powerup.au
www.agilityclick.com/~ial

North American Flyball Association (NAFA)
1400 West Devon Avenue #512
Chicago, IL 60660
Telephone: (800) 318-6312
Fax: (800) 318-6318 www.flyball.org

RESOURCES

Academy of Veterinary Homeopathy (AVH)

P.O. Box 9280
Wilmington, DE 19809
Telephone: (866) 652-1590
Fax: (866) 652-1590
E-mail: office@TheAVH.org
www.theavh.org

American Academy of Veterinary Acupuncture (AAVA)

100 Roscommon Drive, Suite 320
Middletown, CT 06457
Telephone: (860) 635-6300
Fax: (860) 635-6400
E-mail: office@aava.org
www.aava.org

American Animal Hospital Association (AAHA)

P.O. Box 150899
Denver, CO 80215-0899
Telephone: (303) 986-2800
Fax: (303) 986-1700
E-mail: info@aahanet.org
www.aahanet.org/index.cfm

American Holistic Veterinary Medical Association (AHVMA)

2218 Old Emmorton Road
Bel Air, MD 21015
Telephone: (410) 569-0795
Fax: (410) 569-2346
E-mail: office@ahvma.org
www.ahvma.org

American Veterinary Medical Association (AVMA)

1931 North Meacham Road – Suite 100
Schaumburg, IL 60173
Telephone: (847) 925-8070
Fax: (847) 925-1329
E-mail: avmainfo@avma.org
www.avma.org

British Veterinary Association (BVA)

7 Mansfield Street
London
W1G 9NQ
Telephone: 020 7636 6541
Fax: 020 7436 2970
E-mail: bvahq@bva.co.uk
www.bva.co.uk

MISCELLANEOUS

Association of Pet Dog Trainers (APDT)

150 Executive Center Drive Box 35
Greenville, SC 29615
Telephone: (800) PET-DOGS
Fax: (864) 331-0767
E-mail: information@apdt.com
www.apdt.com

Delta Society

875 124th Ave NE, Suite 101
Bellevue, WA 98005
Telephone: (425) 226-7357
Fax: (425) 235-1076
E-mail: info@deltasociety.org
www.deltasociety.org

Therapy Dogs International (TDI)

88 Bartley Road
Flanders, NJ 07836
Telephone: (973) 252-9800
Fax: (973) 252-7171
E-mail: tdi@gti.net
www.tdi-dog.org

PUBLICATIONS

BOOKS

Lane, Dick, and Neil Ewart.
A-Z of Dog Diseases & Health Problems.
New York: Howell Books, 1997.

Rubenstein, Eliza, and Shari
Kalina. *The Adoption Option: Choosing and Raising the Shelter Dog for You.* New York: Howell Books, 1996.

Serpell, James. *The Domestic Dog: Its Evolution, Behaviour and Interactions with People.* Cambridge: Cambridge University Press, 1995.

MAGAZINES

AKC Family Dog
American Kennel Club
260 Madison Avenue
New York, NY 10016
Telephone: (800) 490-5675
E-mail: familydog@akc.org
www.akc.org/pubs/familydog

AKC Gazette
American Kennel Club
260 Madison Avenue
New York, NY 10016
Telephone: (800) 533-7323
E-mail: gazette@akc.org
www.akc.org/pubs/gazette

Dog & Kennel
Pet Publishing, Inc.
7-L Dundas Circle
Greensboro, NC 27407
Telephone: (336) 292-4272
Fax: (336) 292-4272
E-mail: info@petpublishing.com
www.dogandkennel.com

Dog Fancy
Subscription Department
P.O. Box 53264
Boulder, CO 80322-3264
Telephone: (800) 365-4421
E-mail: barkback@dogfancy.com
www.dogfancy.com

Dogs Monthly
Ascot House
High Street, Ascot,
Berkshire SL5 7JG
United Kingdom
Telephone: 0870 730 8433
Fax: 0870 730 8431
E-mail: admin@rtc-

associates.freeserve.co.uk
www.corsini.co.uk/dogsmonthly

WEBSITES

Dog-Play
www.dog-play.com/ethics.html
A cornucopia of information and pertinent links on responsible dog breeding.

The Dog Speaks
www.thedogspeaks.com
Canine Behaviorist Deb Duncan's site, filled with useful advice on canine etiquette, behavior problems, communication, and relevant links.

Petfinder
www.petfinder.org
Search shelters and rescue groups for adoptable pets.

BIBLIOGRAPHY

Billinghurst, Ian.
Give Your Dog a Bone. Self, 1993.

Coren, Stanley.
The Intelligence of Dogs: A Guide to the Thoughts, Emotions, and Inner Lives of our Canine Companions. New York: Bantam Books, 1995.

Lee, Rawdon B.
A History and Description of the Modern Dogs of Great Britain and Ireland. H. Cox, 1899.

DEDICATION
To Johnny and Justin, with love.

ACKNOWLEDGMENTS

My gratitude goes to Barbara Pendleton, who introduced me to Poodle grooming when I was just a teenager. Her time, patience, and kindness will never be forgotten. I'd like to thank my good friend, Jill Pawl Krentz, for allowing me to practice my grooming skills on her Toy Poodle, Snowy, so many years ago. And thanks to my parents, Clint and Jeanne Backes, who supported me in opening my own grooming salon. Without these people, I might never have had the chance to meet all the wonderful Poodles I've loved over the years.

ABOUT THE AUTHOR

Janice Biniok is a member of the Dog Writers Association of America and has written numerous articles on companion animals. She devoted many years to operating a dog grooming salon where her favorite "people" were Poodles. She now combines her English degree with 30 years of experience training, grooming, and caring for animals to produce written resources for pet owners.

PHOTO CREDITS

Photo on page 51 courtesy of Mary Bloom.

Photos on pages 6, 12, 38, 49, 153, and 164 courtesy of Paulette Braun.

Photos on pages 143 and 146 courtesy of Judith E. Strom.

All other photos courtesy of Isabelle Francais.

Nylabone® Cares.

Millions of dogs of all ages, breeds, and sizes have enjoyed our world-famous chew bones—but we're not just bones! Nylabone®, the leader in responsible animal care for over 50 years, devotes the same care and attention to our many other award-winning, high-quality, innovative products. Your dog will love them — and so will you!

Toys   Treats   Chews   Crates   Grooming